Ron is a warm and caring gentleman with a homespun Midwest charm that's infectious and captivating. He also knows his stuff.

Ron's words perfectly captured the fears, the dreams, and the struggles I had experienced as a nonprofit leader. I'm sure you, as a reader, will have the same response.

The tips located within these pages are golden. They come from years of experience working with nonprofits who have lived through mistakes, mishaps, and misjudgments, thus missing the money form generous donors.

Whether you're relatively new to the fundraising profession or even if you've been in the trenches Raising money for some time, Ron's book should be required reading.

I think you'll agree after reading this book that Ron Rescigno has hit the mark.

George Boodrookas, Ed.D.
Owner, Philanthropia Consulting
Modesto, CA

Self-proclaimed watchdog organizations would have you believe that donors care mostly about your numbers, but what donors really care about is the impact of the work you do and knowing how their donations made a difference in the lives of people (or animals or the environment). Ron elaborates on one of the most important aspects of fundraising in his book – stewardship. It's a must read for anyone in fundraising.

Adam Woodworth
Executive Director, Children's Museum in Oak Lawn

Ron's book is like a strategic field guide for fixing fundraising mistakes that keep organizations from raising the kinds of revenue that would be truly difference-making. So read it and keep it handy for the next time someone asks, "Why aren't you raising more money?"

Amy McMahon
Head of School, Rosary High School

OMG! Ron's nailed it!!! I'm so excited for his message to get out. So much of his book is what major gift work is all about. I highly recommend Ron's book. If followed, this book will dramatically improve your fundraising efforts. As a 30-year fundraiser, I can tell you it's practical and easy to follow with huge impact! Ron's made a truly special sauce to add to your fundraising mixture.

Jacqueline S Joines
Senior Fundraising Consultant

If you've been meaning to improve your fundraising efforts but just haven't gotten around to it, Ron's book is a collection of lessons that will hone your skills and turn you into an authority. He brings humor and experience together to give us sound pieces of advice.

Adam Woodworth
Mary Grace Wolf, Co-founder Innovative Fundraising

This book is a roadmap for fundraisers, offering tried-and-tested examples of storytelling techniques to build lasting donor relationships. Ron's approach simplifies how to effectively create urgency and communicate impact, making it accessible for any fundraiser to fold into their strategy.

Renee Davis
Senior Fundraising Consultant

FATAL
FUNDRAISING FLAWS:
HOW FUNDRAISING MISTAKES, MISHAPS, AND MISJUDGMENTS CAUSE YOUR NONPROFIT TO MISS THE MONEY

RON RESCIGNO

FATAL FUNDRAISING FLAWS:
HOW FUNDRAISING MISTAKES, MISHAPS, AND MISJUDGMENTS CAUSE YOUR NONPROFIT TO MISS THE MONEY

For more information, please visit www.ronrescigno.com

Cover by DG Marco Alvarez & Layout by LDG Manuel Serna
Published by Fig Factor Media, LLC | www.figfactormedia.com

Printed in the United States of America

ISBN: 978-1-959989-81-3

**FIG
FACTOR
MEDIA**

DEDICATION

This book is dedicated to my wife, best friend, and business partner (and the president and CEO of Rescigno's), Sue Rescigno. You started Rescigno's back in 1992 out of a sincere desire to help nonprofits raise more money for their important causes. When you first told me about your idea for a business, I thought you were many things: crazy, naïve, and a dreamer among them. Well, thank God for the dreamers in this world. Over the last thirty-one years, Rescigno's has helped numerous nonprofits raise over $100 million and counting. You believed in what I thought at the time was a passing fancy—a business you could call your own.

You also believed in me and that I could help you make Rescigno's a success. In fact, you believed in me more than I believed in myself. And for that, I'm oh so grateful.

TABLE OF CONTENTS:

FOREWORD

I had eight years under my belt as the executive director of the Modesto Junior College Foundation when I first met Ron Rescigno. He called me on the telephone in 2019 after attending a conference on community college advancement. I was serving as a volunteer board member and president of the Network of California Community College Foundations. I was working with colleagues throughout the state, mostly in small fundraising shops, who were struggling through the issues of growth and sustainability for their foundations.

Ron's words impressed me. How could I not be impressed? Ron is a warm and caring gentleman with a homespun Midwest charm that's infectious and captivating. He also knows his stuff. By the end of that initial call, I was very open to Ron's business proposition about how I could help my organization and perhaps others.

I was already familiar with the importance of the annual fund as the lifeblood of our nonprofit. I was also aware that donor acquisition, cultivation, and stewardship were critical pieces of the annual fund approach for our foundation. I had gained much knowledge from a mentor, David Barnes, an award-winning copywriter for political campaigns and nationally recognized nonprofit organizations for over fifty years. I understood the power of well-crafted direct mail letters and emails to help us reach and engage our alumni and donors. Using those media, we were steeped in alumni story gathering and storytelling and, as a result, gathering donors to our cause.

Sadly, my mentor's health was failing quickly, and not long after, he passed away. Ron's call was very well timed, as I had been contemplating how to continue on the positive path my mentor had helped us take.

I could tell instantly that Ron and his wife Sue were true professionals and that their Rescigno's team could help us elevate our annual fund to the next level. Around that time, we were getting serious about a comprehensive campaign for the college to coincide with our 100th anniversary.

Ron and Sue became our guides. Along with our campaign counsel, they worked with us to craft an even better direct mail and donor stewardship program. They helped us make sense of our donor wealth screening data and even designed our collateral materials for the campaign. They also understood the power of story and how it can influence donors' behavior, turning them into partners in support of the cause. Everything we produced with the help of the Rescigno's was touched by the story.

Thanks to the Rescigno's team and our generous donors and volunteers, we reached our $10M campaign goal during the college's centennial celebration. I happily retired as we were wrapping up the campaign and began my consulting business in August 2022. I now refer my clients to Ron and Sue for their annual fund development needs.

When I read the manuscript of Ron's book, my nonprofit life flashed before my eyes. Ron's words perfectly captured the fears, the dreams, and the struggles I had experienced as a nonprofit leader. I'm sure you, as a reader, will have the same response. The tips located within these pages are golden. They come from years of experience working with nonprofits who have lived through mistakes, mishaps, and misjudgments, thus missing the money from generous donors. I wish I'd read such a book when I began my fundraising career. I might have avoided some of the pitfalls. Fortunately, my mentor and my guides helped me avoid some of them . . . or fished me out once I was heading down the pit!

Whether you're relatively new to the fundraising profession or even if you've been in the trenches raising money for some time, Ron's book should be required reading. I certainly will be referring my clients to this book and the concepts within it to help them improve their practice.

Now, more than ever, we need mentors, partners, and information sources that help us cut through the irrelevant and cut to the chase of the fundraising mission. We have serious work to do impacting our communities. I think you'll agree after reading this book that Ron Rescigno has hit the mark. After all, as a fundraising professional, it really doesn't matter what your mission is; you have serious, even critical, work to do to make a tangible difference for your cause. This material will make that difference for your nonprofit.

Enjoy the book, and best wishes on your efforts to improve the impact of your work.

George Boodrookas, Ed.D.
Owner, Philanthropia Consulting
Modesto, CA

INTRODUCTION

The reason nonprofit organizations exist is to do good in the world. If you're reading this book, you'll probably agree with that statement.

They see a problem and look to solve it. They exist to improve the lives of vulnerable people or animals, protect the environment, empower folks like you and me to do better and give us what is needed for our survival. This being the case, then **why would an organization whose only real purpose is to do good in the world fail?** This book will discuss some of the reasons for that failure and reveal some of the ways to achieve greater success in your fundraising efforts.

In 2015, Ben Carson, who, in many polls, was running a close second to Donald Trump for the GOP presidential nomination, claimed that "nine out of ten nonprofits fail." An exaggeration, to be sure. In fact, data from the National Center on Charitable Statistics reports that approximately 30% of nonprofits fail to exist after ten years.

In response, the National Clearinghouse of Data for the nonprofit sector in the U.S. suggested that nonprofits have greater longevity than Carson's statement would lead his followers to believe. The point I want to make here, though, is **nonprofits do fail.** That's been my main motivation for writing this book—not the fact that they fail, but what they (and you) can do to raise more money for the important causes each of you serve.

According to *Forbes*, over half of all nonprofits that fail or are in a state of "no growth" can point to leadership issues and the lack of a well-thought-out fundraising plan. These are two of the issues I'll be addressing in this book.

The philanthropy research group, Candid and the Center for Disaster Philanthropy, has reported that "more than one-third of U.S. nonprofits were in jeopardy of closing within two years because of the financial harm inflicted by the viral pandemic." A sobering thought, if ever there was one, I would say. At the same time, you would have to be very naïve or just plain living with your head in the sand to be surprised by this, wouldn't you agree?

The March 2021 study also underscored the perils for nonprofits whose monetary needs have escalated over the past couple of years despite the unprecedented donations received from individuals and foundations during the pandemic. The point is that sometimes bad things happen to good people and organizations. Maybe this has been the case at your nonprofit. If this sounds pretty dire, it is!

The answer to avoiding these consequences, of course, is to increase support substantially. And while it may be true that arts and entertainment organizations may be at the greatest risk, nonprofits from all sectors are in danger. If your nonprofit has reduced costs by narrowing its focus or by laying off fundraising staff, you're even more vulnerable.

Can nonprofits turn previous failures into future success? Yes, they can. But saying or wishing it to be true isn't enough. **In this book, I will address the most common mistakes fundraising departments make and provide strategies or a plan of action to fix or avoid them altogether.**

What this book is not meant to do is help you maintain the status quo or simply keep up with your competition. After thirty-two years of working with nonprofit organizations, I'm tired of talking to development professionals who aren't interested in growing their support. They're satisfied or complacent. I'm not. I want to help you do more, raise more money, and make great things happen for those you help.

I'm betting that if you're reading this book, you are one of those who aspires to do more than what you did last year. As Pat Riley, five-time world champion NBA head coach, once said, "If you're not getting better, you're getting worse." And if you're not improving, you're destined to be bogged down by the same problems and issues that plague other organizations. I want to help you be aspirational in your approach to raising more support so that you can have an even greater impact. In short, I would like to play a part in you and your team being more successful in raising money for your organization.

This book will address some of the most common failures that I have experienced while working with nonprofits and offer suggestions and tips that will allow you to innovate, execute, and deliver better overall results in the revenue that you raise.

INVESTMENT
IN THE FUNDRAISING PROGRAM

CHAPTER 1
REFUSAL TO INVEST IN SUCCESS

"Efficiency" and "low overhead" are golden calves in the nonprofit world, but becoming obsessed with these goals can make them into idols."

—Philanthropy Daily, March 2022

A woman I met at a conference during the Great Recession of 2008-2009 said something to me that I've never forgotten. I remember her words well, not only because of what she said, but because of what I should have but didn't say in response. She and I were making small talk outside of one of the rooms where an educational session would be beginning soon when I mentioned that Rescigno's Fundraising Professionals helps nonprofits with such things as fundraising strategy, the annual fund, major gift programs, communications to donors, donor retention, etc.

It turned out that she happened to be an executive director. What she said that I've never forgotten was this: *"You'd be proud of me. I have cut my organization's expenses quite a bit."* When I asked her what she meant by "quite a bit," she said *"Well, I've slashed expenses by 30%."* She went on to say that she was proud of the projects she had "slashed" and the staff she had laid off. She was also proud of the fact that her board had commended her at the last board meeting for the vastly lowered expenses. That told me a lot right there.

She visibly lit up when she said fundraising and communications were the two areas she cut the most. She went on to say that, at the current time, there was no fundraising or marketing happening. None. Zero. You get where I'm going with this, right?

After about 30 seconds of stunned silence on my part, I asked her to share what was going on with the work they did. When she gave me a quizzical look, I said, *"You know, what's happening with the reason your nonprofit exists? What's happening with your everyday work?"* She said, *"Oh, we're not doing much at all, but because our operating expenses are so low, everything's fine."*

Talk about being satisfied! Talk about a cushy leadership position!

You know how sometimes, after an incident occurs, you think about it and say, "I wish I'd said . . .?" Well, that was me that day. I blew an opportunity. I should have said, *"Don't you know you're never going to grow by cutting your expenses? You're going to be stagnant. If you're not growing, you're going to wither up and die."* But I didn't. If that lady reads these words, her ears are probably burning.

Let me say this: to a degree, I understand what she thought she was doing. I used to be a principal at a small, inner-city Catholic high school in Chicago. The school was in danger of closing because of low enrollment and high expenses. I had the nasty experience of having to significantly cut the budget, which meant getting rid of programs like music appreciation, band, home economics, art, and all sports programs. I had to let some talented teachers go, too. But I only did it to get enough room in the budget to grow. My cuts were to balance the budget so I would have some dollars to invest in growth.

The woman I talked to at the conference didn't know it then, but she was the poster child for the saying, *if you're not growing, you're dying.* I can't say it any more plainly than that.

If you're a leader and your organization is already stagnant or in decline, doing nothing will not improve things. Not even a little. You'd better be thinking about making drastic changes to get the resources you need to grow. If you do have to make difficult decisions regarding budget and cutting expenses, cut just enough to have resources left to invest in growth.

In fundraising, cutting expenses does not lead to growth. **Investing does,** however. Find a way to invest in future opportunities. And I'm not talking about future opportunities three years from now. Rather, I'm talking about three months, or better yet, three weeks from now.

You may be wondering what the cost of lack of investment is in human terms. It's my experience that the best, most talented people in your organization won't stay. If these people see budget cuts that allow you to merely survive without providing for growth through investment, they'll have their resumes out sooner than you think and be out the door in the blink of an eye. That's because the best people in your organization want growth and excitement, not the fear of being let go at any moment.

Unfortunately, from a leadership perspective, this kind of short-term thinking leads many talented development professionals on what has become a merry-go-round of moving from one job to the next every two to three years.

I don't know who you are, but it's an educated guess on my part that there are probably as many of you reading this who have been at your nonprofit organization for less than two years as there are those who have been there for more than two years. My point here, is nonprofit organizations that have a constant turnover in staff are the ones most in danger of not showing any growth. After all, building relationships that matter usually take more than two years. And that's very sad.

Professionals jumping from one organization to another signal to donors a lack of consistency and little or no growth because relationships aren't being formed. And while it's true that Americans are obsessed with doing more with less, you should know that when donors, especially high-end donors, choose which causes they want to support, they first look at how much is being spent needlessly.

Getting by on the smallest budget possible without skimping on salaries, staffing, and equipment isn't easy. In fact, it's downright very difficult. And yet, far too often, nonprofits make the decision to forgo things they need, such as upgrading their computers, in favor of looking as lean as possible. Phooey to that! As a fundraiser, you're responsible for producing results. Too often, though, you aren't given the tools necessary to do the job. Does any of this sound familiar?

A question for you: who is overseeing your fundraising program? Is it your finance director, your board chair, your CEO, or president who makes decisions? Is the idea of investing in fundraising something you know you should do or is it something the "higher-ups" won't allow you to do?

In early 2021, I had a conversation with a development director of a private college. I asked her if she would like to talk about how her annual fund was performing. She asked if I was trying to sell her something, which I guess

I was—**our "Proven Process" for annual fund success.** But before I could answer her, she said to me, "Look, I already know that you have to spend money to make money, but you need to have money to spend it and we don't." Ironic, isn't it, that in the for-profit world, no one questions this basic business principle? I wished her well and moved on with my day.

I don't need to get hit over the head. I've been working with clients long enough to realize that there are organizations that just don't have the necessary financial resources to grow their fundraising programs and, barring some kind of financial windfall, never will. However, I also know that the "no money" argument is often a bargaining ploy to see how much a company like Rescigno's will reduce its prices if they play the "poor us" card often enough and loud enough.

"Oh, we'd like to work with you, but blah and blah and blah," is the usual refrain.

In the old days, we'd slash our prices just to get the work. And you know what? Almost every time, that client would be the biggest pain in the neck you could imagine. Excuse my honesty, but that's just how it was and still is most of the time.

I also know that there are some nonprofits who are just plain satisfied with "steady as she goes." One development director friend of mine related the following to me:

> When I started with this office, I made it a point to arrive by 7:30 every morning. If I needed to stay late, I would. I wanted the boss to know that I was ready for this job. Now that I'm the development director, everyone comes in at 9:00 a.m. and leaves at 5:00 on the dot. There's just not the same energy or enthusiasm. I don't get it. Does the work get done? Yes. But where is the drive to do more, to excel?

This attitude is a direct result of a refusal to invest in the development office. People, sooner than later, figure out that they don't have to do more. What the heck? The higher-ups are "satisfied," so why bother trying to do more! Dangerous thinking; very dangerous.

WHAT WE'VE LEARNED OVER TIME

Rescigno's has learned a few things since those early days. Heck, we've been in business for thirty-one years, so we better have learned something along the way. For example, we've learned that if an organization finds value in who we are and what we bring to the fundraising table, they will find the money that will allow us, or a company like ours, to help them.

I can't tell you the number of times we've said goodbye to potential clients who said they had "no budget" only to have them call us back a month or two later to say that they moved some things around and now had the funds to invest in whatever it is—a direct mail annual fund program, welcome packets, a donor retention plan, major donor direct mail, you name it. Would it be too much of a stretch to assert that one of the chief reasons nonprofit organizations fail when it comes to raising the money they need to survive, much less flourish, is investment? No, not at all.

Maybe this organizational short-term thinking shouldn't have been as much of a surprise to me as it was. If you're thinking that his particular "fundraising failure" isn't necessarily your fault, I get it. You may be trying to make miracles happen on a shoestring budget. Raise your hand if you've thought to yourself that if you and your staff just work harder and put in more time, great things could happen.

But you know what? That's when burnout happens! If

your nonprofit is always on the verge of disaster or merely getting along, but not growing, I feel your pain. I hope this isn't the situation you're in, but if it is, it may be time to get your resume together. Sorry, but that's the cold, hard truth.

Does your board or CEO chirp in your ear that growth will have to come without investment? Horrors! And close to impossible to accomplish, too.

Are any of these scenarios familiar to you?

- You're expected to work miracles with very little budget.
- Your board expects you to work hard with little in the way of compensation for you or your staff.
- The tools you have to work with are outdated.
- You're asked to save whenever and wherever you can.
- You're forced to look for the least expensive solutions to challenges or problems instead of the best solutions.
- You don't dare "invest" time or energy in anything until your big event is over.

Just nod if you've ever been told that you can't do your fall or end-of-year appeal or newsletter because the postage is too much. Instead, you're directed to simply do an e-appeal or e-newsletter because it's so inexpensive.

A moment ago, I mentioned that some fundraising failures aren't your fault. However, where does your responsibility begin when it comes to bearing the burden of educating "the higher-ups" as to what it takes to run an effective development office and raise more money?

That's a bit of a hard, and maybe even uncomfortable, question to answer, isn't it? Perhaps it's one you don't feel qualified to answer, or you've talked about it, but it's fallen on deaf ears. If that's the case, maybe you can bring in someone from outside your organization who can give your board or CEO an impartial third-party perspective.

When I've had this conversation with chief executives or boards, the main point I make is quite simple and direct: When a nonprofit fails to invest in funding, in effect, it decides to stunt the organization's potential for growth.

It's not uncommon for many organizations that raise a million dollars or more to have an underperforming website or weak financial plan. If you think hiring a trained professional to carve out a fundraising plan or redesign a website might seem extravagant, not doing so can lead to a painful downward spiral or even stagnation.

Nonprofit leaders must be made to understand that high, or even moderate fundraising costs, are an investment. If that investment is not made, the organization's future growth will be very impaired. This is very serious stuff and must be treated as such.

Some nonprofit executives, like the one I referenced earlier, brag about their "low overhead." They think it's a badge of honor. It's not. They actually advertise in their impact reports that "0% of donor contributions go to fundraising costs."

If you're guilty of similar language, stop it. It's counterproductive. Instead, talk/communicate with your donors and other constituents about the impact you're having relative to your allotted budget.

Imagine going into Dunkin' Donuts and ordering a coffee that costs $2.50. Imagine announcing that you only want to pay for the coffee, but nothing else associated with it, not the cup it comes in, nor the time it took someone to make the coffee or pour it for you. In other words, "I don't want to pay for your overhead. I'll pay $1.75, but that's it."

Good luck with that.

Similarly, if the above scenario describes your organization, what you're doing is perpetuating and encouraging a mentality where success is measured by how little you spend rather than on the impact your spending has on the lives of those you serve. Remember, your nonprofit is a business and should be run as one.

Here's my solution: you must invest in technology, talented staff, and professional development if you wish to raise more money. That's what you should be doing. Convince the powers that be at your organization to find the money and give them a visionary picture of what an increase in budget will allow you to do.

Again, if your nonprofit is of the mindset that miracles will happen with little or no investment, you've got a problem. Admit it, aren't you more than just a little bit sick and tired of substituting more and more hard work for staff time and money? I don't blame you for feeling that way.

Organizations need to stop cheating themselves by scrimping. The **more you scrimp, the less you raise.** Stop wasting the time and energy of your most precious resource—your people. You should also be investing in a first-rate donor management system. Find the best one that works for you, not the one that's least expensive. After all, the bottom line means everything to your nonprofit, as does making efficient operations and cash management essential ingredients of success.

A donor management system can reduce expenses and overhead and make it possible for a single worker to achieve what previously may have required your whole team's attention. From a donor's point of view, the reality as I see it, is that they're:

- Easily forgotten.
- Not respected nearly enough.
- Not given enough grateful appreciation and recognition.
- Often not even thanked.

And yes, I'm certain that if more time, energy, and money were spent on the creation of excellent donor experiences, they would stay longer and you would raise more funds. And I can assure you that your increase in income will be more than what you spend on those donor experiences.

Remember, the experiences you give your donors result in donor loyalty and eventually donor retention. Don't hold back investing fully in those experiences. They are the key to building long-lasting relationships.

Finally, there are many reasons why nonprofits fail when it comes to raising the money they need to survive, much less thrive. Chief among them, however, is not investing in the growth of their programs.

It boils down to this: *Investing in fundraising is very likely the most effective investment your organization can, or ever will, make.*

> "When nonprofit leadership begins to understand that high fundraising costs are an investment in future fundraising success and that the failure to do so seriously impacts its ability to expand and grow, that's when you'll be able to do great things."

As a development professional, you're in the business of asking people to fund your mission. Regardless of the economy, your organization makes the world a better place. That is a constant that is worth investing in.

And from the donor's viewpoint, I would encourage you to help them see what they are helping you to achieve rather than what you are spending.

CHAPTER 2
THE WHEN TO HIRE THE DOD DILEMMA

"The power of human empathy, leading to collective action, saves lives, and frees prisoners. Ordinary people, whose personal well-being and security are assured, join together in huge numbers to save people they do not know and will never meet."

—J.K. Rowling, author

It's no secret that development positions have a high turnover rate. In fact, development director roles are often known as "watch 'em come, watch 'em go," as these individual cycle in and out of organizations at alarming rates.

Noted author and president of Cygnus Applied Research, Inc., Penelope Burk, conducted a study which found that it is common for fundraisers to stay at their jobs for about sixteen months before leaving. Let me repeat that: Sixteen months or little more than a year. And, of course, replacing them is neither easy nor inexpensive. In addition, it most certainly creates a great burden for organizations that depend on strong relationships with their donors.

Put bluntly, this high turnover means big-time trouble when it comes to financial support. Overwhelmingly, individuals who have been in their current positions for longer periods are more successful than those who come and go so quicky. Much more. It only makes sense, too.

Why the high turnover? I believe that unrealistic expectations significantly damage the morale of development staff. I've seen it far too often to think otherwise. According to one study, 75% of chief development officers and 62% of CEOs felt that "unrealistic expectations" was the number one culprit when it came to high turnover[1]. *(Benefactor, March 2021)*

Over the past thirty-one years, we've worked with our fair share of smaller nonprofits who ask us if the time is right to hire a director of development, and if they do hire one, how long it will be before the position pays for itself. When I hear this, I immediately think to myself, "Uh oh, that's the wrong question." It's also the wrong thought process in that it indicates that the organization is more concerned with how much the new person will cost for a year rather than what the long-term positive effects of the right hire will be. Specifically, **the question that should be asked is this: Is my organization ready to make the commitment necessary to ensure the success of the position?**

I understand the feelings of many in development when it comes to feeling like they're not adequately compensated for late nights, and tight deadlines, and their ability to balance being analytical and creative, assertive, yet warm and outgoing, as well as insightful. There's no doubt in my mind that the position is a challenge, for sure. Add to this the fact that many find themselves disconnected from the rest of their organization's

---

[1] Benefactor, *Stop the Revolving Door in Nonprofit Development*. Ronald Guisinger, March 24, 2021.

operations. Think about yourself for a second: do the various departments at your nonprofit work together or share information the way you think they should?

If I've heard it once, I've heard it a thousand times when meeting with development professionals:

- Marketing has their data, and they won't share it with us.
- Marketing has stories, but those are their stories, we don't have access to them; we have to find our own.

Here are some considerations you need to think about to decide if you're truly ready to hire a development director.

Which fundraising activities will take up the most time?'

1. Special events?
2. Donor engagement?
3. Direct mail appeals?
4. Donor calls/visits?
5. Database management?

Vital to fundraising success is the proper balance of the time required for each of these activities and so many more. When it comes to responsibility for making these kinds of decisions. there must be an understanding of where your support comes from. Let me give you an example:

The general public assumes that institutions are the primary supporters of nonprofits. *The reality, however, is that individual donors account for more than two-thirds of nonprofit support, while eleven percent comes from foundations and only four percent comes from corporations.*[2]

[2] Philanthropy.iupui.edu, Latest Data Shows New Low in Share of Americans Who Donated to Charity. July 27, 2021.

What that strongly implies to me, is that if your organization spends the majority of its time writing proposals and chasing after grants from foundations, you may very well be disappointed and, by the way, you will not have built the structure necessary for a comprehensive fundraising program.

What about your board of directors? For far too many nonprofits, it's an "us vs. them" mentality. That is really unfortunate because fundraising success demands a board that fully participates in the fundraising process, and depending on your role, it may be up to you to train those members.

If your board "fully participates," bravo! If not, maybe it considers fundraising the responsibility of staff and no one else. Or maybe you've got a well-meaning board, but their understanding of what it takes to be successful in fundraising is limited.

If your board expects the staff to handle all fundraising and simply asks for reports at board meetings, you may feel like you're dodging a bullet. In one narrow sense, I understand. However, from a larger perspective, not only does board participation in fundraising improve the chances of your success, but it's also a sign of how healthy and advanced your program is.

When Rescigno's has worked with organizations whose boards are involved in development planning, have the tools they need to play their part, and receive staff support, they usually have a well-put-together, high-powered development program. If so, that's when you can be pretty sure that you're ready to hire a director of development.

There is one thing that shouldn't be forgotten: the importance of budgeting money for development above and beyond the salary of the new hire. Too often, an organization adds a director of development but fails to give the person the funds necessary for such things as fundraising technology and other ancillary materials.

Think about it:
- Donor records must be kept.
- Gifts have to be accurately recorded.
- The information must be tracked.
- Files have to be merged for mailings.
- Thank-you notes need to be generated.
- Communication pieces need to be printed and mailed.

Without the tools necessary to perform these rudimentary fundraising tasks, even the "development director of the decade" will likely fail.

Let's revisit the original question posed in this chapter: *Is your organization ready to hire a director of development, and if so, how long will it take for that position to pay for itself?*

You probably are ready for this kind of hire if you've got an engaged board, a commitment to building a strong donor base, funding for the position for more than one or two years, and your programs are strong enough to add an additional, qualified staff position that will contribute to raising more money.

CHAPTER 3

THE "LET'S LEAVE WELL ENOUGH ALONE" LEADERSHIP MISTAKE

"If we merely aim for the industry standard, then our goal is mediocrity. Emulating the average nonprofit, we are destined to live with all of the problems the average nonprofit faces . . . aim to be exceptional in your approach to fund development."

—Eddie Thompson, Thompson & Associates

I'm assuming that you agree with my chapter one premise that a failure to invest in what it takes to raise more money is, in effect, really accepting, even welcoming, less than stellar participation from those who could be supporting you at greater levels than they are currently.

I've alluded to the fact that nonprofits who are struggling usually have a problem that starts at the executive level. Executives who dislike the idea of fundraising are deadly to their organizations. What they insure, especially at small nonprofits, is that they stay small and underfunded.

If you're an executive and hate fundraising, you are holding your organization back from raising more money and doing even better for others. If, on the other hand, you love your organization and what it does, you shouldn't be settling for what some call complacency (while others use the term mediocrity or just plain laziness). This syndrome I refer to is a killer of innovation. In a way, it's a disease, and it's contagious. If you feel your program is stuck in the past and has become complacent, you're not alone. If you fear taking a risk because it might jeopardize your success, guess what—you're moving backward, not forward.

A lack of investment isn't the only reason nonprofits fail or do poorly when it comes to raising money. I've seen many good organizations struggle to raise the money they need because they're stuck in a quagmire of disorganization, lack of focus, and disarray.

In October of '22, Sue Rescigno, my wife, partner, and CEO at Rescigno's, and I attended a conference for community colleges (CASE). We were talking to an executive director who said his college has done very well with its annual fund and didn't need any help. We were about to congratulate him (in fact, I think we did) when, almost as an afterthought, he said, "But we haven't grown very much either."

It was like a light bulb went off in his head! When this well-meaning gentleman heard those words come out of his own mouth, he didn't need us to tell him something wasn't right. "Doing very well" and "haven't grown very much" don't exactly go together like, say, bread and butter, now do they? We've since been consulting with him and his team on different parts of the annual fund that they had ignored for far too long.

Is it time for you to say, "That's it! I'm sick and tired of getting the same old results. I'm not going to take it anymore?"

As a professional fundraiser, I'll bet you're inundated with suggestions from everywhere when it comes to ideas for raising more money. Has a board member or maybe even your boss ever come up to you and said, "I just heard that Oprah gave a million dollars to The Holy Mother of All That's Holy Mission. Have you tried contacting her?" Well-meaning? Sure. Misguided? Of course. Totally! The problem with this mindset, or the one that says *we're doing okay just as we are, so let's not try anything new, is that you'll get the same poor or "okay" results.*

But what about if you want more than that? What then? I contend that the number one skill today's fundraiser can have is curiosity about learning what it takes to be successful at fundraising.

At a recent Association of Fundraising Professionals conference, it was reported that the fundraising profession will face a talent crisis in the coming years if there isn't an investment made in educating young professionals entering the fundraising sector. One of the recommendations made at that time included developing a new set of standards that included the levels of knowledge needed to be a fundraiser. I love that idea, by the way. The profession needs curiosity seekers.

Walt Disney once said, "We keep moving forward, opening new doors and doing new things, because we're curious, and curiosity keeps leading us down new paths."

I don't know about you, but I try to read something related to fundraising every day. I want to know what others think about the issues that confront us. I try to stay abreast of the latest trends. It's a priority. And I share what I learn with Sue and the rest of our team, as they do with me. When it's pertinent information that our clients would benefit from, we include them in that sharing of knowledge.

During my thirty-two years in fundraising, I've been privileged to work with boards and chief executives with a true passion for fundraising. I've also experienced boards and executive teams where one or both were complacent or even downright negative when it came to raising money.

I once met with a president and chairman of the board of a religious organization whose contacts were vital to the success of a major donor direct mail campaign we were starting. I stressed the importance of their value as donors to this effort and the support I was hoping for from their contacts and friends. Separately, both said the same thing: "Ron, as a board member, I'm a volunteer. Isn't that enough?" Well, no, it's not because as a board member, your financial support is also expected.

I have found that staff and volunteers understand the role fundraising plays in a nonprofit's ability to provide services when leadership is role modeling in a positive way and sharing the good news and successes of the work you do. After all, shouldn't everyone have a vested interest in their organization's fundraising success?

On the other hand, when leadership doesn't believe in the essential nature of raising money, well, it just makes your job so much harder. And when it comes to asking for and receiving big gifts and renewing gifts, there is simply no substitute for donors knowing and trusting the staff leader. Even at relatively modest levels, donors want to know and trust the person responsible for spending their gift in accordance with their wishes and the nonprofit's mission. If you're an ED who has turned the fundraising task over to other staff and volunteers, you've greatly reduced your organization's likelihood of success. As an ED, you're the face of your nonprofit and critical to its success with fundraising.

I work with a private high school whose development director is great. She works hard and has done a great job at the school for many years. She told me she would be retiring at the end of the year. During her years at this school, she's been saddled with a president who doesn't like to ask people for money. In fact, he doesn't like to meet with people either. Can you imagine how difficult that's been for her?

She called me to thank me for all Rescigno's has helped her accomplish in terms of raising much-needed funds. I asked her if she was sure she was ready to call it a day, and she said that, yes, she was done, mainly because of the lack of support from her president.

No matter how many fundraisers are on your staff, **the CEO must play a significant role in the fundraising effort.** If you're asking or wondering why, think about it. Some donors expect and want to be asked by the highest-ranking person in the organization. Call it misplaced pride or hubris, but this is one of those cases where it is what it is. Plus, a strong CEO often goes along with an equally strong board. The advantage to this is that it increases donor confidence in the results or impact their support will make happen.

The chief executive must understand the need for a strong fundraising program. And it's his or her responsibility to ensure the board is "on board," too. When this doesn't happen, poor performance is almost always the result.

> *"I don't ask anyone for money. That's not dignified for someone in my position. That's why I have staff." (Anonymous president of a private educational institution)*

How can you speed up this process for an organization that is wishy-washy about fundraising? Staff and board members should participate in educational programs like workshops or even retreats led by professionals. The agendas of board and staff meetings should regularly include reports about special events, new initiatives, and fundraising successes.

Involving board members and staff as volunteers in planning direct mail campaigns, solicitations, and other development activities could be beneficial to your efforts to stop poor results and that old bugaboo complacency. The bottom line is, does the concept of everyone buying into the importance of fundraising start at the top and work its way down at your office? It should. It must. Why? Because that's what is meant by an organization having a culture of philanthropy.

Everyone understanding how the organization's financial health is stronger because of fundraising success goes a long way in inspiring everyone to feel they have a real stake in promoting and participating in the work you and your staff do. Are you and your organization willing to accept poor results? As I've already said, when this kind of mindset is prevalent, it can be very dangerous. It can impact the quality of employees you hire, how you set your goals, and how you measure success.

Rescigno's has worked with some wonderful nonprofits whose progress was stunted because they were forced to hire less-than-ideal major gift officers, or data specialists, or well, you name it. And believe this: executive directors who are nice people but fundraising averse should no more be in a leadership position than Bugs Bunny should be POTUS.

I'm reminded of something I heard or read long ago: *garbage men get used to the smell of bad garbage.* Have you become so accustomed to the smell of poor performance that you and your team are satisfied with underperformance?

With all that being said, let me ask you the following: Are you doing the same thing you did last year with your fundraising program? I'm talking about things like:

- Using the same appeal as you sent out two years ago.
- Mailing to the same list you always mail to.
- Failing to segment.
- Ignoring data clean-up and de-duping.
- Doing only one direct mail appeal.
- Failing to ask for specific gifts.
- Failing to send a prompt, personal thank you.
- Failing to have a donor communication plan in place that supports retention.
- Failing to do donor acquisition.
- Lacking knowledge of your donor retention rates.

- Failing to have specific goals for all aspects of your fundraising program.

As I mentioned earlier, the bullet points above are very much like a disease to a nonprofit because they kill innovation and drain energy. And it's an easy disease to catch. I call it the disease of satisfaction or the complacency I referred to earlier. For example, are you afraid of trying something new for fear that it might jeopardize some of your past successes? If you're guilty of this disease, guess what—you're already dying. Get moving forward. You'll be glad you did.

I promise you I haven't made this up, and I've got to tell it. In November of '22, I called a nonprofit's development office. I got an automated voicemail (no real person answering the phone), which said, and I quote, "At this time, we will not be accepting any more donations until the beginning of the new year." I wanted to laugh until what I really wanted to do was cry a million tears.

I was flabbergasted at the thought that a nonprofit would greet callers with that kind of recorded message. There was no explanation why they weren't accepting any more donations and would not be until the new year, which was nearly a month and a half away.

Don't misunderstand me, though. This nonprofit, a shelter for homeless and abused women, may have had a perfectly good reason for being unable to accept any more donations. But did the recorded message actually mean they would accept no donations at all, or did it mean no donations of food or clothing or other actual "things"? What if I were someone wanting to ask how I might make a monetary donation? Did the recorded message mean they would not be accepting those either?

I think you see my point. I could have been ready to send them a check for who knows how much, but their recorded message, in essence, said they didn't want my money. Not "at this time," anyway. Couldn't they, ct the very least, have said something like, "If you would like to make a monetary donation, you may do so by doing this, that, or the other thing?

What about *your* crganization or your department? Do you feel you've been pulled into mediocrity? If you want to overcome it, a deliberate and continuous *investment* (there's that word agair!) of focused energy on areas that ensure that you are constantly moving towards excellence is necessary. That pull towards leaving well enough alone is a strong one. Fight against it. As cn old acquaintance of mine once said, "The longer you sit, the longer you want to sit." So, get up and make the changes that get you headed toward constant improvement.

CHAPTER 4

NON-CHANGE MAKERS—THE ARCHITECTS OF DECAY AT YOUR OFFICE

"The change we dread most may contain our salvation."

—Barbara Kingsolver, American novelist, and poet

As I mentioned earlier, Walt Disney once said, "We keep moving forward, opening new doors, and doing new things because we're curious, and curiosity keeps leading us down new paths."

Change can be a good thing as long as you don't let it take you down dead-end paths (rather than the new ones Mr. Disney was referring to). Heck, if Rescigno's hadn't changed during the Great Recession, we'd be out of business by now. Back then, we weren't the full-service consultancy we are today. Our desire to be more than a direct mail fulfillment company motivated us to do more and be more.

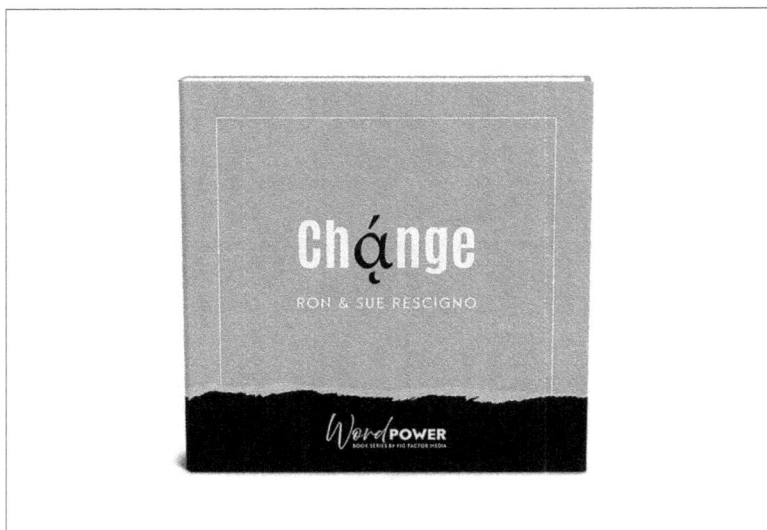

There can be no disputing the fact that fundraising is in a time of change, especially since COVID-19. More and more often, when donors make a gift, they are responding online to appeals made through traditional methods, like direct mail. That's why it's more difficult to know how well certain campaigns are doing. At first glance, it may look like you've received a disappointing response to a mailing that ends up being a big success because there's been a split between those who gave by mail and those who went online to respond. You must know this is happening. If you don't, you're going to want to (or be encouraged to) cut direct mail spending. When you do that, you'll end up losing both mail and online responses.

Does your nonprofit have a structure that hinders clear thinking about this issue? It's quite possible because many organizations are very siloed in their approaches. The people who do direct mail want their share of credit since they are triggering gifts that come online and through mail. The problem is that the digital department doesn't necessarily report to development but to marketing. So, when the digital department makes statements like "online revenue is up 58%!" what they probably should more accurately be saying is online giving skewed direct mail results by 27%."

There's no turning back to the old days about this, and that's a good thing. It's the way donors have shown us they want to respond to appeals. Old ways won't open new doors.

But here is what you can do to make the best of this situation:

- Place all fundraising functions, including online, under one office. Direct mail won't survive without online giving and vice versa. The channels must learn to work and survive together.

- Get help from professionals when it comes to results across various channels. If you don't, it's pretty much a given that you'll make bad decisions or assumptions about how you raise money.

- Have a conversation with your chief executive about what makes fundraising communications different. Take the time to explain that while marketing and communications are focused on reporting past successes, fundraising must be focused on what outcomes may result from future fundraising.

- Talk to your marketing and communications colleagues and learn about their needs.

- You need good stories that make your donors feel warm and fuzzy about the support they provide your cause. The marketing team also needs them. Try very hard to develop an inter-departmental story team focused on identifying stories, doing interviews, and beginning to create a bank of stories for your organization.

If there's resistance to change, you may not be able to get any of the above items done. Hence, the title of this chapter. I don't know about you, but I can feel a resistance to change when I merely walk into some advancement offices.

Sue and I once went into an educational institution's district foundation office and wondered if we'd ever find our way back out to our car. I mean, it was at the very end of a long, dark hallway. Certainly not a very inviting place for a donor or potential donor to come for a visit with the executive director. If your department is located in a back office somewhere, think about the message you're sending to potential visitors. In case you're wondering, the message is your department is an afterthought instead of the primary driving force for good at your school, or healthcare institution, or you name it. Come to think about it, what does it say to the rest of the employees at your organization? It says, at least to me, that fundraising is an afterthought and not something to be respected.

If this is true at your nonprofit, you need to work to change that perception immediately.

There have also been many occasions when we were brought into an office with only the executive director's desk in it. At smaller nonprofits, that's understandable. Space may be a legitimate issue. But I'm talking about mid-sized or larger nonprofits that deem it okay to put their fundraising staff in extremely cramped quarters. It's disrespectful to the people who bring in the money. It really is. It speaks to the importance (or lack of importance) the organization places on fundraising, and it can give off a feeling of desolation, despair, or even hopelessness. Do you think I'm overstating this? I don't.

"I've heard the words", "Well, we've always done it that way," many, many times. Let me echo the words of character actor Brett Goldstein, aka Roy Kent, of the hit Apple TV series *Ted Lasso*: "No, that's dumb!"

Just because things have always been done in a certain way, does that mean that change is bad? I don't think so. Not at all. To improve or grow a fundraising program, things *should* be changing. Does that change always have to be major? No. I can tell you this with a great deal of certainty. I've never worked with any nonprofit organization whose systems were so perfect,

NO, THAT'S DUMB

so finely tuned, that there wasn't at least some room for improvement.

Stop saying you intend to continue doing things as they've always been done. Unless you've brought in all the revenue your organization will ever need, "That's dumb!" You may be asking yourself what's the best your nonprofit can ever hope to be if they're unwilling to improve or change. In my estimation, the answer is "mediocre," and if that is what is happening at your place, then you're dying a slow death whether you want to admit it or not.

Right now, change is all around you. Hundreds, maybe even thousands, of executive directors have left their positions since the pandemic. As of March 2023, COVID-19 had been with us for three years and counting. This has been a period of great change for fundraising, yet more is needed. Whether we like it or not, "change" or doing things differently is a prerequisite for remaining relevant and productive.

> *"Progress is impossible without change, and those who cannot change their minds cannot change anything."*
> —George Bernard Shaw

Maybe you or someone you know is in a comfort zone of being reluctant or afraid to change. If you're doing everything right, then the need to change is not so urgent. That's quite a standard to live up to, though, right? Who among us is doing every single thing right? Certainly not me!

If you accept the premise that there is room for change, then what's stopping you? Is it, in fact, the person you see when you look in the mirror? How often have you been guilty of saying, "That's just how we like to do it?"

Maybe you haven't said it out loud, but you've thought it. If this describes you, you're hurting your nonprofit's ability to grow and do more good in the world

Here is a list of "non-change maker" symptoms that might help you:

- You don't talk to fundraisers from other organizations.
- You don't attend conferences to learn more about your profession.
- You don't hire fundraisers because you perceive them to be a threat to your position.
- You're not interested in testing what works and what doesn't.
- You think it's below you to talk with donors.
- You won't listen to or invite expert advice.
- You won't confront your colleagues in marketing who aren't writing in a donor-focused fashion.
- You're not really interested in analyzing the results of your work.
- You refuse to go to your boss to get more budget and staff to support your goals and objectives.
- You refuse to accept blame when results are poor; it's always someone else's fault.
- You make few, if any, attempts to motivate colleagues.
- You have no plan for communicating with your donors.

Unfortunately, fundraisers guilty of some of the above symptoms of "refusal to change" are not often held accountable. They stay in their role for years and years, doing the same old thing time after time. And those are the very fundraisers who never have enough funds to care for those they're supposed to serve. If you recognize these symptoms in yourself, is it time for a change? Of course, it is. Do you have the courage and fortitude to set a plan to move forward?

PLANNING **FOR SUCCESS**

CHAPTER 5

A GOAL WITHOUT A PLAN IS JUST A WISH

"Give me six hours to chop down a tree, and I will spend the first four sharpening the ax."

—Abraham Lincoln, 16th president of the U.S.

Those who know Sue know that she's the planner in the family. For example, before we take any trip, even if it's to a place we know well, she researches the latest restaurants, places of interest, and entertainment. She makes restaurant reservations well in advance and puts together an itinerary of possibilities to make sure we take advantage of our time away.

I, on the other hand, like to improvise and explore. A plan? Who needs it? That was me until a few years ago. We had just arrived on the Caribbean Island of St. Maarten. It was probably 8:00 p.m. or so local time. Sue had asked me before booking the flight what time I'd like to arrive there, and I said, "How about just before it gets dark?" She said, "Are you sure you don't want to get there earlier? We've never been there and won't know where we're going." "Nah," I said, "let's just wing it. It'll be an adventure."

Well, by the time we got our rental car, it was already dark. It was supposed to be about a fifteen-minute ride up a mountain to get to our resort. What could go wrong? Roundabouts, that's what. Image of a Roundabout The directions seemed easy enough except for the fact that neither of us had any experience with navigating roundabouts. If you've never experienced one, a roundabout is a circular intersection where drivers travel counterclockwise around a central island. I'm still a bit confused whenever I come across one. There are no traffic signals or stop signs. In the U.S., I later learned, these are known as traffic circles.

Now, I've driven in Sicily before. The rule of law there is when you come to a stop sign, you beep your horn and just keep going. That was a picnic compared to trying to make our way through what seemed like a series of disconnected mazes. It was now pitch black out, and Sue was doing something unusual. She wasn't saying a word. We were lost, and we knew it. We knew we were close, but we just couldn't find our resort.

After a couple of hours of aimless driving, Sue finally broke her silence. She said, "Ron, let's just go back to the airport and sleep there tonight. We'll find our place in the morning." No way were we going to do that because our flight was the last to land or take off that day. The airport was closed until morning, and it wasn't like there were any hotels attached to the airport like there are in big cities.

I learned my lesson. While being adventurous and not having a plan may seem exciting, it really created a bit of a dangerous (and avoidable) situation for us. Finally, as we continued to roam aimlessly, we asked a motorist if she knew where our resort was, and she said, "Yes, it's right there beyond that gate. Just press the button on the gate, identify yourself, and they'll let you in."

If I had taken the time to look into the directions to our resort beforehand, I would have known that we were going to be experiencing something we were unfamiliar with—roundabouts—and been able to plan for it. The lesson to take from this near fiasco is that having a plan can help you when it comes to being able to cope with the day-to-day realities you face in real-life situations—and in fundraising, too.

When you stop to think about it, whether the work you do is with major or annual giving donors, what you should be doing is building relationships. Having a plan to do so (and not just "winging it") is really important.

And by the way, I know many nonprofits who host a gala or auction in the spring, a golf tournament in the fall, a luncheon in May, and then send out a year-end appeal in December. This is not a plan. It's a series of strategies strung together throughout the calendar year with little or no thought to what happens before and after these events. Namely, how do we engage these donors in our mission? In addition to solicitation strategies, the best fundraising plan includes outreach, engagement education, stewardship, retention, and ongoing board development.

Why a Plan? Providing donors with communications, between appeals and without making another ask, that connects them to their impact is what turns occasional donors into loyal ones. A thoughtful plan for doing so, is vital if you want to do it well.

For some time now, there has been a good deal of research that leaves little doubt that after donors send their gifts they want/need to know what the impact of that gift was. By providing donors with this kind of systematic and well-thought-out sequence of communications, you are building up their knowledge and familiarity with your organization while, at the same time, winning their trust, which, in turn, improves loyalty.

And it's very important that your board has ownership of the fundraising plan. If only the staff (or you) are involved in the writing, overseeing, and implementing of the plan, they will be the only ones who are invested in its outcome. To be clear, this is not good. You want everyone on your team to buy into the plan.

If yours is like most nonprofit organizations, the annual giving program is the basic revenue generator for your mission. A written plan makes it understandable, easy to measure, and achievable. It should be a plan that predicts income at certain times during the year based on solicitations that will be happening. The annual giving income part of the plan is for the organization's current needs, though not always just unrestricted.

In determining the goals, you should start with the data—who gives, how much, and how often. This should help you pinpoint the strength of donor loyalty, how well your donor acquisition is doing, as well as leadership giving strengths and weaknesses. This is also where you can see areas needing improvement in donor retention and other areas needing tweaking.

Donor recognition should definitely be a part of your plan, especially if donor retention at your organization is under 45%. You should always be re-assessing your donor appreciation, communication, and recognition efforts to deepen their connection with you once they've made a gift.

I'm often asked just what exactly makes for a successful donor communication plan:

- **After the gift** – The easiest place to start a donor communication plan is what you communicate after the gift has been received. This is the stewardship and communication phase of your plan. It would include a thank you letter, tax receipt, a new donor welcome packet, and phone calls. What's important is that you and your team know exactly what gets sent to which donors and when.

- **Communicating through the seasons** – These are the communications that can help you stay in touch with donors through meaningful updates. This might include newsletters, gratitude reports, impact reports, handwritten notes, etc. Remember to space these communications out so they don't interfere with your asks.

- **Impactful content** – The best donor communication plans are clear in messaging and outline what you will be sharing with your donors. Stories make for really meaningful content in donor communications.

- **Channels that work best for you and your donors** – You need to know how you'll share content with your donors. Start by honoring donor preference regarding digital or direct mail communication. You'll have to take into consideration your organization's budget, time, and resources to deliver different types of communications.

- **Deadlines** – Good fundraising plans include steps for your development strategies with deadlines for each step. Deadlines keep everyone working at the correct pace.

- **Responsibilities** – Who on your team is responsible for what?

You may be wondering which should come first. The writing of the plan or the creation of a budget. In other words, should an organization write the plan first with a goal of raising as much as possible, and then develop a budget based on the plan, or should the organization write out its budget for programs and overhead first, and then write a fundraising plan to meet the goals the budget lays out? I believe the best way is to develop your program budget first, and then write a fundraising plan to meet its goals. I have learned that when nonprofits write the plan first, they often end up with a bunch of unrealistic revenue goals. When nonprofits write their budgets based on unrealistic goals, everyone ends up being disappointed.

So, develop the budget and then write a fundraising plan to meet its needs. Be honest when it comes to your organization's capacity. This is why when Rescigno's is asked to come in and help with an organization's needs, we first ask if they have a budget to accomplish their goals rather than asking to see the plan first. There's no use going any further in discussions if the budget won't allow for goals to be met (as discussed in the book's first and second chapters).

CHAPTER 6

WHY YOU NEED A FUNDRAISING PLAN . . . NOW

Plans fail for lack of counsel, but with many advisors they succeed.

—Proverbs 15:22

You've got a list of things to do that's longer than there are hours in a day to complete them. Everyone needs something from you before the end of the day, or they're predicting disaster. You, in turn, feel the pressure of getting things done, so they're off your plate. You had a to-do list, but now it's nowhere to be found. Meanwhile, the "busy work" just keeps piling up.

When you go to bed at night, do you ever hear the following echoing in your brain as you try to get some sleep? *"Why aren't we raising more money than we did last year?"* If this is an accurate description of how you feel more often than not, I understand. Everything's got to be done NOW is no way to go through your fundraising life.

What's really happening most of the time is this: **You're too busy mopping the floor to turn off the faucet.** So what happens is the sink in the kitchen overflows because you never quite get to the faucet to turn the water off (which is now on its way to your living room and the new carpet you bought just a month ago).

Here's the sad part: no matter how much or how furiously you mop, you can never make any headway because you aren't able to get to the source of the problem—in this analogy the faucet in the kitchen sink. If this describes how you feel, it could be a case of not having a fundraising plan that you stick to (or having a plan that's just not very good).

Many nonprofits, particularly smaller ones, have no plan. We've seen it often. These are organizations who more or less fly by the seat of their pants. When someone has an idea for an event or a campaign, they put together a committee or volunteer group, and off they go. There may be a letter that goes out about the new initiative or a donor meeting or two that is held. Then, when the bank account is really low, panic is the name of the game. That's when everyone runs around trying to find cash to keep the doors open. Obviously, that's not the best way to run a development program, wouldn't you agree?

And even if you feel like you have no money problems, if you're fundraising operation is unorganized AND has no plan, that's a recipe for fundraising disaster.

The best thing this type of nonprofit can do is have a written fundraising plan in place. It doesn't matter whether the organization is a church, a school, or how far along they are in their operations. They need a comprehensive, well-thought-out, and written plan for fundraising. A plan that will allow them to focus their efforts, plan out a yearly fundraising calendar, and be a guide for strategy and tactics when they are in the middle of events, mailings, and donor calls. In short, a good fundraising plan will keep these organizations from going crazy in the day-to-day madness that can exist in a development office.

THE WHO AND WHEN OF A PLAN

If you feel like you've been mopping like crazy for the last few years, think about what you can do to improve things NOW and then what you can do next. My strong hunch is that you'll love the results.

Who should write your plan, and when should it be written? Let me answer the second question first. As I alluded to above, your plan should be written now— it really is worth the time and effort even if it means dedicating a week to get it done. As for who should write the plan, if you've got a development director, that person should write it in consultation with the executive director and other staff members or board members who can offer input. If you don't have a development director, then the ED should do it. We have been asked on more than a few occasions to write plans for different organizations, which we're happy to do in consultation with them.

It's very important to know the end goal when starting to write a plan. This "end goal" isn't something you just come up with. It should be based on your needs. How much money will your nonprofit need to raise in order to successfully carry out the activities you want to perform in the coming year? If the goal answers the question "How much money do you need?" then your mission should naturally answer the question "Why do you need it?" In other words, what do you plan to do with the money you raise?

Once you know how much you need to raise and why you need to raise it, it's time to figure out how you're going to raise that particular amount. What tactics will you use to reach your goal for the coming year? Your plan should go into detail at this point. You can do this by figuring out a goal for each tactic. For example, if you need to raise $100,000, you may say you will raise $70,000 through major donors and $30,000 from an event. Other common tactics may include:

- Individual Giving
- Major Donor Groups
- Events
- Direct Mail
- Online and email giving
- Grants
- Corporate Giving
- Annual Giving

It's now time to create a timeline. You've come up with a budget, you have a great mission, and you've drawn up a plan that includes various fundraising tactics. This is where you must be careful because if you fail to set timelines, you'll never seem to get things accomplished.

I know plenty of veteran development professionals who prefer general timelines. Hold an event in March, send out a couple of mailings in the fall, that sort of thing. I, however, like more detailed timelines that go beyond simply listing big-picture goals. I recommend listing all of the small goals that go into making the big goal a reality. Instead of just listing that there will be an event in March, go into detail. Specifically state when decisions need to be made on venue and entertainment, when sponsors will be solicited, and when invitations should go out.

The bottom line is that creating a timeline will force you to think carefully through your fundraising decisions and provide you with invaluable guidance on activities as you go through the course of a fundraising season.

CHAPTER 7

NOT DIGGING DEEP ENOUGH TO FIND OUT "WHY" YOUR DONORS GIVE

"Before you start some work, always ask yourself this question: Why am I doing it?"

—Chanakya, ancient Indian teacher

I once made a presentation at a church workshop where I asked attendees, "Why is fundraising so important for your church and its members?" For the most part, the audience's response was to "help pay the bills." When I followed up by asking if fundraising to pay the bills was going well, there was a general shuffling of feet and looking down. The reaction reinforced for me an important lesson: People don't develop a habit of giving based on what an organization needs.

Inviting people to give their gifts to God or any good cause, for that matter, must be about the "why." Why should giving be so important to your donors? Do you know why your most loyal donors support you? Have you ever taken the time to simply listen to what they have to say? Maybe you have, and the answer was, "Well, I continue to give because of the excellent work you do." Did you just accept that answer without digging any deeper?

When I talk to prospective clients, I'm constantly surprised at how many annual fund programs have flatlined. Year after year, overall revenue barely increases. That doesn't always mean they don't have good donor retention rates. In some cases, they do. What it does mean, however, is donors aren't moving up or increasing their giving. And that's not good.

Last year, I spoke with a development director who said, "Our donors just don't seem to have any affinity or capacity to give more. We've done wealth screenings, and though they give regularly, they don't increase their giving very much at all."

She shared with me the name of one donor who certainly had the potential to give more than he was currently. I asked her if she had any thoughts on why the donor wasn't increasing his giving. Her answer was, "Well, I think it's because..." I stopped her right there. I said, "You think, or you know?" That right there, is the problem.

You've got to care enough to find out what your donors' passions, interests, and motivations are. Especially those donors who have been loyal but haven't increased their gifts. You could be so much better at what you do if you would add this to your repertoire of activities. It's almost a sure thing. Take the time to start asking your donors "why" more often, and you'll be surprised at what you find out. The answers you receive could lead to some great clues and even "wow" moments where you learn more about your donors and why they choose to be connected to your organization.

To say it another way, if you don't know the answer to "why" your donors give to your organization, you're not giving yourself a fair shot at more support and success.

I've often been asked how to get someone who is giving five thousand dollars a year to take the next step. I always reply, "Do you know why that donor gives to you so regularly? What's his story?" As I said earlier, the answer should not be, "I'm not sure." Knowing why your donors support your organization's work is vital. It will result in you making informed decisions about how to treat and appeal to them properly.

Believe me when I tell you that if you unlock this key bit of information from these donors, both the relationship and the money will take off. When you find out about your donors' passions, interests, and motivations, you'll understand and know their reasons for supporting your cause. When you do, inspiring them to give more will be much easier.

Some questions that you may want to ask your donors to find out more about them:

- What types of issues either in the community or the world are you most interested in or most troubled by?

- Have you ever supported a nonprofit before? Did the organization do a good job of making you feel good about that support?

- Was there a time when you supported an organization, and they didn't make you feel good about the support you were giving them?

- Would you be interested in learning how to get more involved in our organization?

- Does it take time and determination to take this extra step? Yes. But if you don't, you'll never reach the next plateau of fundraising success, guaranteed!

MESSAGING

CHAPTER 8

COMMUNICATING RESULTS, NOT ACTIVITIES

". . . Whatever result may reveal,
Failure or success,
But feel yourself blessed!!
No result is an ending,
Just a new beginning!"

—**Mansi Kolecha, scientist**

I made mention of administrative costs in chapter 1 of this book with my example of Dunkin' Donuts and overhead costs. I'd like to amplify on that.

A fundraising campaign for a cultural organization came to my attention in 2021. They sent a solicitation to their donors whose theme was "unity," hoping to position themselves in such a way that when the pandemic ended, people would once again be ready to gather at in-person events. The organization touted its impact and the milestones t had reached. The problem was their materials were focused on numbers and, therefore, came off as impersonal. Like the number of social media views they'd had during the last eighteen months and the number of times their QR code had been scanned. Not to say that these weren't impressive, but there was no mention of results or outcomes.

Their campaign was all about seeking support to make it possible to "sustain a path of unity," but never explained why unity now, more than ever, was important. All I could determine from the mailing I received was that my gift would show "unity" with others. Nothing was mentioned about how a real person's life had been so impacted that she signed up for art lessons, or how a student's family was brought closer together because of a shared experience. In other words, it was all about activities and nothing about the results of the activities.

Does your nonprofit confuse the two in their marketing and fundraising efforts? Activities are the different things your organization does or provides. Results are the differences made by those things you provide. What you want to do is commit to making your results the priority. Results are the difference or impact made by your activities.

Make no mistake: the work nonprofits do, the work you do, is a tremendous asset to society. As I said in the previous chapter, it's fine that you let everyone know about the important work that you do. But if you get better at talking about why you do what you do, people will have a better understanding of why their support is so important.

If your organization is guilty of silence after a donor's first $1,000 gift, that's just another example of a communication mistake. It's the perfect time to communicate the results you were able to achieve because of the gift.

One example: A successful, middle-aged businessperson working in a tech-related field told me about her experience with a nonprofit. This lady is a philanthropist in the making. She is serious about the support she gives, but also simply loves the idea of giving. I'll call her Donna.

She was aware of a nonprofit in her city that feeds and shelters homeless and vulnerable women. The city's downtown area is near and dear to Donna's heart. She loves the nightlife in the area and really cares deeply for those who are experiencing poverty. The cause, therefore, aligns perfectly with one of her passions.

A friend of Donna's recently began work at the mission. Great connection, right? Donna gave this mission an online gift of $1,000 during the Christmas season. The email acknowledgment of the gift came almost immediately. There was a brief thank you and confirmation of the credit card transaction. Then she heard nothing from them . . . for days and days.

And then, stop me if you've heard this before—after twenty-one days, an email arrived from the same mission asking for another gift. To put it mildly, Donna was disillusioned.

She hadn't really paid attention to the fact that she hadn't received a receipt in the mail and that there had been no communication of any kind since the first email acknowledgment that her $1,000 gift had been received. It was only when she got that next email ask that she realized she hadn't heard from them. She called it a "too quick ask" and explained that it made her feel unappreciated and like she was just a means to an end—money.

She told me, "They haven't even asked me why gave the first gift. All they know about me is my credit card number. How can they possibly know if I can afford a second gift? Why would they make that assumption?" At this point, I should share with you that Donna was a new, unsolicited donor. She wasn't even in the organization's donor database.

Think about the implications:

- What could a gift of that size be telling the nonprofit about the donor's capacity to give?
- Was there a bigger opportunity waiting to see how the nonprofit responds?

And then put yourself in that donor's shoes. How would you feel if you had given $1,000 of your hard-earned money to this organization, and the only communication you've had from them is an automatic acknowledgment and then, three weeks later, a request to give more? I don't know about you, but I'd be thinking, "Forget them."

And then consider what a donor is entitled to. I assume you agree with me that it's more than what this donor received, especially if you hope to grow a relationship with her. Maybe you're quite satisfied with that one-time gift of $1,000, and you don't care if you get another gift or not. If so, then just go right on and ignore the opportunity to grow the relationship. I would just ask you one question: Are you really doing that well? Or are you just lazy? I suppose that's two questions, but you get my point.

If you are serious about finding out more about this person and developing a relationship, then take the next step by thanking the new donor as personally as you can and, while doing so, make sure that you confirm for the donor that the gift was important and making a difference in someone's life. This process of "making real" what the gift accomplished is a truly important and often overlooked step when it comes to communicating with donors after a gift.

Here's an example of making a gift's impact (a donor's impact) real:

"Thank you so much. Let me tell you about one woman who is now off the streets because of your generosity."

Then you can tell the story in a couple of sentences, offer a tour (virtual or in-person), and close the communication, be it an email or a phone call, with heartfelt thanks and offer to answer any questions. **To me, that's how you at least begin to build a relationship.**

Something to think about: Is there a process at your nonprofit that notifies you or whoever the right person is, who will then take the right action after that big first gift has arrived? For your cause, the threshold may be $1,000; for others, it might be $500. Whatever that level is, there needs to be a process.

This is important: If anyone in your data or accounting departments or anyone else says it's not possible to develop and keep to a process, insist that it's imperative to grow funding, because it is. I have faith in you. Get this done.

The naysayers will offer you every excuse they can think of:

- "In the fourth quarter, we get so many gifts to process; now you want us to be looking out for new gifts at *what* level? Impossible!"
- "At the beginning of the new year, we're still trying to get through all the gifts that are still coming in daily."
- "We've only got two people to process the gifts. How can you expect us to . . ."

I've heard them all before. So have you. Stop enabling

the behavior is all I can tell you. The simple fact is you must make a big deal of any first gift that comes in at a certain level, whatever you designate that to be. When I say make a big deal, I mean you must make sure you are treating any first-time donor well, but especially those who give at certain pre-designated levels.

If you ask around to some of your colleagues at other nonprofits, you'll find that $1,000 gifts aren't all that rare, though I would assume they're not an everyday occurrence. My point is that when you get one, you need to be ready to build the relationship through proper communication. My suggestion for you is to come up with a way to easily communicate with new donors in such a way as to make sure they understand the importance of their decision to make such a generous gift to your cause.

As I mentioned, you should tell a story of a person whose life has been changed because of the donor's generosity. Have the story ready. Then, you have to figure out how you're going to know who your new donors are. Can you get a list of them every week or month (if you don't have too many)? How will you contact them? Will it be email, phone, or some other method? Once you've got this figured out, work out the plan.

I am sure that if you begin to think more like a donor, more income will come your way.

CHAPTER 9

THE STATISTICAL TEMPTATION TO AVOID IN YOUR COMMUNICATIONS

It's a lot of work for a donor to read each number, put it in the correct context, and remember it in case they need to know it later in the letter.

—The Better Fundraising Co.

One of the ways Rescigno's helps organizations raise more money is by helping them see that they're using too many numbers in their appeals, both direct mail and email varieties.

Here is an example where I emphasize the numbers by...

The Membership for All of Us program provides low-income families with a special spa membership at a greatly reduced rate of $20. This is a program that supports families who are income-qualified and living in dangerous situations to exercise, play, and learn just as anybody else would, with the same benefits as any other membership we offer, like the one you had.

Our goal is to serve 3,000 families through our Membership for All of Us program. We are currently over 1,500, with a 140% growth over the last three years. Remember, this initiative is supported by individuals and organizations in our community to help offset membership costs. Donor support for this program ranges from $1,000 to $5,000.

That amounts to two paragraphs with eight separate numbers that I've underlined. And please notice that a couple of the numbers are spelled out. Also, there are dollar amounts and a percentage to factor in with the numerals and words. That's a lot, especially when you consider that those different numbers represent gift ranges, membership rates, and goals.

This organization's intentions were well-meaning when they put the above together. They believed that by including these numbers, the donor would better understand the situation and be more likely to give a gift. What they didn't take into consideration, however, is the fact that it's a lot of work to read all of the numbers, consider them, and remember them in case they need to know them for later on in the letter. The lesson here is that the more you make a donor do something (like think about numbers), the less likely they will be to finish reading your letter and then send a gift in. **This is exactly why successful direct mail appeals and e-appeals usually have very few numbers attached to them.** This is not to say that numbers should never be used.

Notice that all the numbers below serve to help the donor in the decision-making process. If you take a look at that list, you'll understand my point even more:

- How much will it cost to help one person?
- How many people a donor can help by sending in a gift.

- Gift ask amounts.
- Matching grants.
- This is exactly why a bulleted list like the one below is often used (even though it does have several numbers):
- Your gift of $25 will be doubled to $50 to help 5 people.
- Your gift of $75 will be doubled to $150 to help 20 people.
- Your gift of $200 will be doubled to $400 to help 40 people.

The Magic Number is One!

So, **when it comes to fundraising, one is the magic number.** Not 100 or 1,000, or even 100,000. I've learned over the years that this is a tough lesson to teach. Logically, you would think that donors would respond more positively when you mention how many people you feed, house, educate, heal, etc.

Let's say your nonprofit helps bring clean water to children, shelters the homeless, or rescues animals who have been deserted. The cause really doesn't matter. You might be tempted to say that in a particular place, there are 125,000 children who have no access to clean drinking water. You might then describe to your prospective donors the horrible diseases that can come from unsafe drinking water. Maybe you would include a photo in your appeal letter of hundreds of children in need of fresh drinking water. Then you make the case that your organization is the one best equipped and qualified to provide for safe, life-changing drinking water.

You send your appeal out and wait and wait and wait. After a month or so, you begin to realize that donors are not responding anywhere near as generously as you thought they would (and need them to). You can't understand why your appeal has performed so poorly until you understand that donors give to help a person, not people in general, but someone they identify with. **It's your job to give them that one person they can relate to.**

One study I read told volunteers about a hungry young girl and then tracked how much people were willing to give to help her. Another group of volunteers was told the same story of the hungry young girl but were also given statistics about the hundreds of thousands of others starving. The group with the additional context and statistical data about the hundreds of thousands who were also starving gave about half as much as those who were presented with the needs of just one girl. Can you see what is happening in this scenario? As the numbers grew, the emotional connection was lost.

Can a conclusion be drawn that people seem to think about problems with big numbers as unsolvable? Is it such a big problem that their donation wouldn't have any effect? That's the conclusion I draw in case you're wondering. This should make you want to review your last few appeals. Are you concentrating on a person in need? That's why at Rescigno's, we focus on "the one" story with a photo or photos of a person in need. That's the story we tell, and you should, too.

My recommendation to you is that you study your use of statistics. But don't misunderstand. I'm not implying that you never use statistics. It's not like you should never give some statistical information. But do be aware that when you do, it's not always easy to figure out if you've crossed the line into discouraging donor support.

Tell more stories about individual people in need.

To help you along in this pursuit, here are some components vital for helping you add emotion to your fundraising:

- Focus on one person. A gift of support from donors will help. And remember, the more numbers you add, the more you take away from your reader's ability to "feel" their decision. The donor has to know whose life he or she is changing, what the person looks like, etc.

> *"If I look at the mass, I will never act. If I look at the one, I will."*
> —Mother Theresa

- There's a lot of competition for the attention of your donor. Emotion may well be the one factor that wins you support over other nonprofits. Emotion will stick, stats won't.
- A good story activates the imagination and sparks emotions.
- Lastly, people remember stories, not statistics.

CHAPTER 10

A FRESH APPROACH TO TELLING YOUR STORY

"Show your readers everything, tell them nothing."

—Ernest Hemingway, author

I n this chapter, I'm about to describe time-tested and proven methods to increase revenue from the stories you tell and write about. It will help you get more donors and keep those you already have giving more and for longer periods. But you can't go about it half-heartedly, as some have.

Sue and I and the Rescigno's team are always looking for the common denominator when it comes to successful stories. One of the most revealing things we've learned is that a great differentiator between organizations that tell excellent stories and those that don't are the kinds of stories they choose to tell. Let me qualify that: there are nonprofits that do a poor job of telling stories that still do raise money—but not nearly as much as they could (like the religious institution I referenced in chapter 9).

I have read and critiqued thousands of annual appeals in the last thirty years. Sad to say, but many appeals are really nothing more than newsletters (that "tell," as I referenced in the Hemingway quote to start this chapter) masquerading as appeals on an 8.5 by 11 piece of paper.

What so many appeal writers still don't get is how people respond to stories—emotional stories. Let's dig into this. Being a good storyteller doesn't automatically guarantee fundraising success, but it is certainly a major factor in raising more money. In fact, I have found that successful fundraising offices have something in common: they tell stories that are specifically chosen to compel people to make a gift.

These successful stories give donors an important part or "role" to play. By the end of these kinds of stories, readers clearly understand that by giving, they are not only a part of the story but, more importantly, a part of the solution to the problem posed in the story.

I assume that you already mention your donors both early and often in your communications to them. That's part of the key to successful storytelling. Let's talk about the word "role." Most donors, we have found, prefer to play the role of hero rather than partner, member, or team of supporters, for example. If you want your donors to take action, be it giving, volunteering, or whatever, give them something to do, a role to play. Focus on how the donor's role is crucial to helping the main character in your story. The way most successful organizations do this is by using the word "you" at least two to three times more often than the words "we, us, or our" or the name of your nonprofit. Once this becomes second nature to you, everything you say and everything you write will be donor focused. Do the above regularly, and your donors will begin to see themselves in your communications. That's when they'll be more likely to make a gift.

The second thing you need to do in your stories is a little more difficult to achieve: make the role you want your donor to play in the story specific and compelling.

When you tell donors what their gift will accomplish, be precise:

- Provide a hungry person with a meal.
- Provide one night of shelter from a below-zero night.
- Provide free access to a children's museum for one child.
- Heal one person.
- Pay for one college credit class.

Warning: Asking your donor to "join with us," "support our cause," or "make a gift that will allow us to help them" is nonspecific and very uncompelling. In fact, it's old and stale jargon. I acknowledge that it's not always easy to be specific about what a donor's gift does. To you, trying to speak in generalities about all of the things your program does or accomplishes may seem natural. However, **from a donor's point of view, the specifics are very important.**

That's why I believe that saying something like, "Be the difference for a homeless man in need," brings in much less than saying or writing, "Your gift of $27 will provide a safe refuge for a homeless woman for a week." Remember, being specific about what a donor's gift does or will do will increase the likelihood of receiving it.

"WHAT" AND "WHEN" ARE MORE IMPORTANT THAN "HOW" YOU TELL A STORY

I've alluded to this earlier, but it bears repeating: simply being a good writer does not guarantee appeal writing, much less fundraising success.

When it comes to raising money, you must tell/ write the appropriate story for each of your various donor communications. When I work with clients on their storytelling, I ask them to focus on two things:

1. Stories that make clear that the donor is needed.
2. Stories that explain the difference or impact a gift will have.

> A good exercise is to take a look at a couple of your most recent appeals to determine if they do this. You see, some donors find motivation in giving a gift when they understand that there is a need or problem that has to be addressed or solved. Donors will give when they know the potential impact or difference their gift will make in someone's life. Do you know what type of story to tell and when to tell it? The important question you need to answer is, *are you asking donors for support, or are you reporting back to donors on impact?*

ASKING FOR A GIFT

When asking for a gift in an appeal, you should tell a story of a current need or a story with a problem that a donor has not yet solved. You're inviting donors to become key players in the story by being part of the solution.

In short, an appeal letter that:

1. Discusses an unsolved problem.
2. Features a person or family that needs help.
3. Is incomplete.

That story should be told in your appeals and e-appeals, fundraising events, and in-person asks. The main idea here is that the type of story you tell should be incomplete because the need has not yet been met, or the person or family still needs help.

A story that reports back to the donor in acknowledgment letters and various Stewardship "touches" that:

1. Describes a problem that the donor has helped to solve.
2. Highlights a person whom the donor has helped.
3. Tells a full or completed story.

This kind of story should be told in your newsletters, annual and impact reports, and meetings with major donors. Your goal should be to share a story with an emotional need attached to it. It should also tell your donor what the solution is so she can imagine herself giving a gift and helping to solve the problem. Allow her to see herself as a potential hero. That's powerful stuff!

I see far too many nonprofit appeals that tell completed stories and then ask for a gift. That's backward and counterintuitive. Your appeal shouldn't have a happy ending; it shouldn't have any ending. As I've said, the ending comes in the reporting back after the gift has been received and put to use.

If you want to raise more money, no matter how counter-intuitive it may sound, tell a story that is not finished and ask the donor to finish it with a gift today. For example, "Gloria is homeless and in a very tough way. *Will you please send a gift today that will help her stay in our shelter facility?" Can you see how this is different from the following: "Gloria was homeless and in a very tough way. But thanks to our innovative program that you have made possible through your support, she is doing much, much better. Will you please send in a gift today so that we may continue to help others who are experiencing homelessness?"*

I'm sure you can see the difference between these two examples. In the first, Gloria's story is unfinished, and donors can see that they can play a role in helping Gloria by sending in a gift.

If your appeals have text that says some version of "please support our nonprofit so we can continue all the good work that we do," know this: you are inhibiting giving, plain and simple. Organizations that follow this advice raise more than those that don't. Period.

Here is an example of a letter a client sent out before starting to work with Rescigno's:

When Jayne and her three kids moved from South Dakota to Virginia, she certainly had no expectation that they would end up homeless. She thought she had a new job waiting for her in Virginia Beach and was excited about it. For whatever reason, the job never happened and Jayne and her family were suddenly forced to sleep and shelter in their car.

Her kids, Larry, 11, and Jeanine, 7, worried that their mom wasn't going to be able to continue to take care of them. Where would their next meal come from? Would they ever find a place to live other than the car? That's when Jayne heard about a place called Plots for Jewels (not the real name) and made the courageous decision to call and ask for help. Plots for Jewels welcomed her, and now the family has a place to live as they try to get their lives back on track.

Today, they're still dealing with the traumatic after effects of having lived in their car for two months.

While Jeanine had been withdrawn and sad, she now has a place to call home and is much happier and self-assured. Larry is also getting much-needed support from the Plots for Jewels staff. And Jayne has found a job that allows her to provide for her family.

Over time, the family will transition to independent living because of generous support from people like you. Please help us continue with our important work for more families like Jayne's. Simply return the enclosed card or if you prefer . . .

Is it clear that the family's problem has already been solved and that the donor doesn't have a role to play other than to "continue with our important work"?

The next letter is one we helped them with:

I'd like to share this urgent bit of news with you.

Two weeks ago, I got a telephone call from a very frightened mom telling me that she and her children were in desperate need of help. The mom, Jayne, had finally decided to leave an abusive relationship. But she and her children really had no place to go.

Here at Jewels, these stories are all too common. The need for safe housing and other resources to help homeless moms and their kids is extremely high.

I'm writing to you today because I could use your help. Because of the pandemic, our resources are very thin.

Your $50 gift will provide a night of safety for one child and one mom.

Can I humbly ask you to provide one night, three nights ($150), or 5 nights ($250) of safety? Every night truly does matter and brings a mom and her kids a step closer to feeling and being safe.

In this version, can you see that there is (1) a clear need that has yet to be met, (2) a specific way the donor's gift will help solve the problem, and a clear way for the donor to be the hero by sending in a gift today?

By the way, in the example of these two letters that were sent to the exact same group of donors, the second letter raised nine times more money than the first letter.

To review:

If you're asking for money in an appeal, make sure your letter does the following:

- Tells a story of NEED.
- Specifies what the problem is.
- Explains the problem clearly and simply.
- Uses emotion.
- Explains the solution to the donor.
- States how the donor's gift will provide the solution.
- Asks for the gift today.

Your letter should not tell donors that their gift will help your organization provide the solution or that it will help support the work your organization does. REMEMBER, IT'S NOT ABOUT YOU. It's about those you help. And it's important to make the problem solvable or small enough to appear solvable.

Example: "You can provide fresh, healthy food for a mom and her children for just $65 per night." This works much better than "Please send us your gift. It will help us end hunger in and around our region."

REPORTING BACK

When reporting back to donors on how their money was spent and what good came from their giving, that's when to tell a story of victory or triumph. Explain how the person in the story was helped, or the problem was solved. Explain what the situation was before and what things are like now as a result of the help given by the donor. Make him or her feel like the hero because of the help they provided.

Again, these kinds of stories should be included

in newsletters, e-newsletters, annual reports, impact reports, etc. Remember, this is where you tell the whole or completed story that shows the wonderful transformation your organization was able to help accomplish (but always because of donor support). This is where you lay the foundation for keeping your donors. Why? Because if you never report back to them about what their gifts help to accomplish, can you really expect them to keep sending more gifts?

Remember, give the donor the credit for helping to solve the problem.

Here is an excerpt of a newsletter story, an example of reporting back, that a client sent to donors before they began to work with us:

The Central Dentistry Program offers free lunch and dental care to low-income children and adults who have no insurance or any way to pay for needed care. This service is available in Minnesota, Idaho, and North Dakota.

Because of dedicated volunteers, last year, we were able to provide almost $10 worth of care to patients for every $1 that was invested in the program.

In 2015, our program treated more than 22,000 people. Therefore, these people are no longer fighting the terrible pain of advanced dental issues. In addition, they are overcoming the socio-economic challenges associated with severe dental issues.

While, in theory, all low-income children are covered by insurance in the tri-state area, they are almost twice as likely to have tooth decay as children from higher income families. Disproportionate barriers to receiving this care, however, is a very big problem. There are many reasons why they have difficulty accessing this help, such as finding providers who will accept the insurance.

Notice the following from the excerpt:

- There is no mention of the donor.
- There's quite a bit of medical jargon and numbers being talked about.
- Those kinds of details make readers skip ahead. Is that what you just did? Donors do the same thing.

This is what was sent out after having worked with us:

She Needed and Received an Emergency Root Canal... because of You, She Got It!

Your thoughtful gift has helped to save the smile of 13-year-old Rhonda. The dental work she needed was urgent and you answered the call.

When Rhonda bumped her tooth, it seemed like no big deal. Her mom thought the bruise and swelling would go away soon enough. The pain, however, went from bad to worse rather quickly. Rhonda pleaded with her mom not to send her to school.

Because of your help, though, Rhonda got the help she desperately needed from the Central Dentistry Program.

And it's certainly a good thing she received that help because it turned out that she had nerve damage and an infection . . .

Please notice the following (all of which helps to make this a very effective impact report):

- This report is all about a person, Rhonda, not the program.
- It quickly sums up the need and then credits the donor for meeting the need.
- It specifically gives the donor credit for helping Rhonda.
- The language and paragraphs are simpler and more easily read.

These four bullet points establish for donors that their gifts made a difference. How much more likely do you think a donor will be to give again because of the efficiency of reporting back that the nonprofit has done? Much more likely? I agree!

If, at this point, you're wondering when it would be appropriate to brag to your donors about the great work you're doing, my answer is that donors give to make a difference much more than they give to fund the "greatness" of your work. There's a difference there, and I acknowledge that it is somewhat subtle, but it's a big-time difference as far as I'm concerned. Talk about the impact to the majority of the people you communicate with.

YOUR "GET SUPPORT" STORY

And don't forget, the story you tell throughout all of your various communications is the feeling or overall impression a donor will have of your organization. I call it your "get support" story because, over time, what you're really doing is telling donors, through your stories, that they're needed and that their support, their gifts, make a very real difference in people's lives.

> **The missing link in many nonprofit stories is the failure to share with your donors and others that everything isn't A-Okay. Yes, you heard me right.** Your organization has to be willing to show that it can't succeed without its donors. Or, to put it another way, they need to show that there is a risk of not meeting the needs of those they serve without donor support.

Please notice the distinction I'm making here. I'm not suggesting you bombard your donors and prospects with what your organization needs. Donors are not really all that interested in what your organization needs. They are, however, very interested in helping to meet the needs of the homeless, the food-deprived, those in need of educational services, etc.

I read many donor-communication pieces during the course of a given year. If there is one thing many nonprofits have in common, it's what they're *not* saying:

Hey Bill,

We don't have a handle on this situation. In fact, we haven't been able to take care of many of the individuals who have come to us for help. Our beneficiaries have enormous needs that we haven't quite been able to keep up with.

You might be thinking to yourself, wow, they'll think we're doing a lousy job. It doesn't sound like everything is in order; it does sound like donor intervention could help solve the problem or need. What it is, though, is very, very honest, wouldn't you agree?

If your organization can improve this one aspect of its communications to its donors, you will be doing it and yourself a huge favor.

So, let's take the italicized paragraph above and examine it for a minute:

There is an urgent problem that we haven't solved. We need the support of wonderful people like you to help us address this NOW. Your gift matters and makes a real difference.

What I'm saying here is that nonprofits must be honest with their donors about problems or issues that need solving and stop worrying that they will appear weak, incompetent, or unworthy of support.

If you have trouble conveying that message, feel free to refer to the following tips for honest communication:

- Discuss the urgent problem or complicated issue you want to address and resolve.
- Stress the role you hope the donor will play; not what your organization is doing.
- Confidently share appeals that tell stories of need, and then in newsletters and impact reports, share with your donors the successes or triumphs you've had (because of their support).

If you master the above, you'll be letting your donors know that they play a truly pivotal role in the work you do and that they're needed, and their support is so very important to those you help.

My promise to you is that when you tell a truly compelling story that describes an unmet need or problem that has yet to be solved and offer your donors a role to play in helping to address the need or problem, you will raise lots of money.

And above all else, when it comes to the actual story, be assured of this: if you're not telling your story, you can be sure that your competition is telling theirs.

CHAPTER 11

EMOTION = ACTION ... LOGIC AND REASON = THINKING

"Instead of reason or logic, go with emotion. Tell the story of a real person. Grab my heart by the throat."
—Steve Thomas, American author, and television personality

Canadian neurologist Donald B. Caine once said, "The essential difference between emotion and reason is that emotion leads to action, while reason leads to conclusions." Would you agree that what you want when you reach out to your donors and prospects is, in fact, action rather than a lot of concluding? I hope so.

I've told this story before, but it bears repeating here. We once worked with a very well-known religious institution that raised lots of money but had been stagnant for several years before they hired Rescigno's to re-invigorate annual giving. The VP of Development at this prestigious nonprofit and I used to engage in spirited (no pun intended) conversations on this topic. Every time he wrote his appeal, whether it was for the fall, year-end, spring, or anywhere in between, we'd have the same conversation.

I'd tell him, "Jack (not his real name), you're doing too much educating and not enough inspiring. You need to dumb your letter down and appeal to your readers' hearts instead of their brains." He was having none of it, or to be fair, very little of it. He'd tell me, "My provincial superior and I both agree that our donors are very educated and would be put off, if not downright insulted, if we communicated with them the way you're suggesting."

Oh well, you know what they say about the customer always being right. Too bad. As I mentioned, this religious institution doesn't hurt for money. They get their fair share and then some. We did help them reinvigorate their program by creating a calendar of regular communications, emphasizing the importance of donor retention, and creating a new donor welcome strategy. They could have gotten more, though. Probably a lot more.

Don't be fooled into thinking that presenting carefully reasoned appeals for support are going to help your organization raise boatloads of money. Time after time, it's emotional, passionate appeals that help to change the world and, by the way, pay the bills. So, lead with emotion in your appeals. It's easy to write about logical stuff or what some call 'institutional speak.'

> "What the mind can't remember, the heart never forgets." —Twan Eng Tan

A final word on this subject: In her book, *The Secret Life of the Grown-Up Brain*, Barbara Strauch writes that as you age, you become more right-brained. You have more empathy, and you respond to things more emotionally. I'd say that's absolutely true. I know I used to be able to watch all kinds of physical mayhem in real life, on TV, or at the movies. No longer. "America's Funniest Home Videos" used to be a laugh riot for me, but some of the tumbles they show people taking make me almost feel their pain.

And ever since I became a dad (and as I've grown older), it doesn't take much to make me tear up. Would you agree with me that this is certainly relevant to you as a fundraiser, leader, or manager? After all, when it comes to donors, their brains are aging too.

I was watching a Chicago Blackhawks pre-game ceremony in early 2022. The ceremony was to honor fans currently battling cancer. They call it Hockey Fights Cancer Night. The Purple Carpet event recognizes fans in remission or walking in memory of a loved one who was lost to the disease. As part of the ceremony, before the first puck is dropped at center ice, each of the Blackhawks' players escorted a child battling cancer out onto the ice with them. At the ceremonial puck drop, a 6-year-old girl from a Chicago suburb who was in remission for a few months joined the Blackhawks announcer and former player, Troy Murray, at center ice. Troy, by the way, had also been battling cancer.

Watching the tenderness with which each of the players treated their young person and knowing what that child at such a young age must have gone through brought tears to my eyes. I was sitting in my basement alone at the time. It got me, it really did. I felt it deep inside. I didn't have to think about it either, which is my point.

While most donors tend to be on the older side, I

strongly suggest that you write to them at around the 7th-grade level. As to the objection of my client and friend at the religious institution I referenced a bit ago, my advice then still stands now: *stir the emotions before trying to appeal to your donors on an intellectual level.*

CHAPTER 12

MAKING IT ALL ABOUT THE MONEY

"The small charity that comes from the heart is better than the great charity that comes from the head."

—Ivan Panin, Father of Bible Numerics

L et me speak personally for a bit and do so as a donor about what I don't get nearly enough of from the organizations I support. I want to feel good about what I can give and not guilty for what I can't. What I don't like at all is when I receive messaging that implies or comes right out and blatantly tries to make me feel bad about what I can't give or do for their causes.

Giving is supposed to be a good experience, right? The organizations that make me feel good about my giving are the ones I give more to. Nonprofits that don't send out those good feelings soon cause me to stop my support. How's that for plain and simple?

While this may seem all too obvious, when a cause I care about doesn't understand or recognize this basic truth and assumes things, well, it's a major turn-off. This is an ever-present problem (or so it seems). That's why when one of my favored organizations that I've supported for several years sent me a request for increased yearly giving, I said to myself, "Oh no, they didn't," but, oh yes, they did!

Let me be clear. I wasn't upset that they asked for an increase in my giving; I expected that. I was upset that I was asked for such a large increase in my support and the manner in which I was asked. Their appeal told me about the trouble they were having solving a clear and present problem. They wanted money to help them address the problem. But what they didn't do was acknowledge my past generosity. They also failed to mention how much they appreciated my past support or explain in any real detail why giving to this new problem would be worthwhile for the people they served.

In my mind, they were assuming that because I gave regularly over several years that I must know pretty much all I needed to know to give more. In short, to me, they were saying, "We need money. Please send more of it . . . now!" And they weren't asking for peanuts. I was given three options for giving: (1) 60% more than my last gift, (2) double my last gift, or (3) a 200% increased gift. I stopped and asked myself if anything had occurred between me and this nonprofit that should have made them feel like they deserved what they were asking for.

About the only good thing I could say about this request for more support was that they threw in an obligatory sentence acknowledging that they can only help others because of "loyal donors like me." Great! Maybe I'm too cynical, but it's been my experience that most donors want more of a reason—a bigger, better, or more dire reason—to increase their giving. As I put their request to the side, I thought to myself that they really didn't know me and had never truly made any attempt to reach out to me personally. **Advice: don't just write to donors when you want to ask for more money. Stop asking donors for more if you haven't explained to them what their previous support accomplished.**

Despite the above, I do still like what this organization stands for. Their cause still matters to me. What I've done to express my dissatisfaction with them is point out where I believe they are missing out on opportunities for more support. I don't do this because I want to be thanked more or because I want more acknowledgment of what a great, philanthropic guy I am. I do it because I want them to raise more money, and I'm sure that they could be raising more and keeping their donors for longer periods of time.

CHAPTER 13

NOT STATING THE NEED FOR SUPPORT STRONGLY ENOUGH

"Charity sees the need, not the cause."

—German proverb

I've already made mention of the need and how it relates to fundraising. Now allow me to amplify on it.

While speaking to a group of fundraising professionals at an AFP chapter meeting in Florida, I was asked the following question:

> *Workshops I've attended have taught me that the best appeals cite a clear and present need and that the more pressing the need is, the better. That seems to go against the kind of messaging we send out, which is positive and affirming. Is there a way for me to illustrate our organization's need for financial support without making it sound like so much doom and gloom?*

I loved that question because it allowed me to discuss what a fundraising appeal is and isn't.

My answer, in brief, appears below (verbatim):

First, think about the different kinds of content you send to your constituents in the form of blogs, emails, on your website, social media, and, of course, printed pieces. Undoubtedly, some of that content includes:

- Engagement pieces
- Impact reports
- Asks
- Newsletters
- Educational pieces
- Invitations to events

I could name more, but I think you understand my point. Each of these communication touchpoints should serve a purpose. The fundraising appeals you produce are the result of all the hard work you've put into your communications. When sent to existing donors, it's very likely they have seen and read what has come beforehand. If you've done a good job with stewardship, when donors read your appeal, they already feel pretty good because of the way you have thanked them for their past support and updated them with impact stories.

All of those "touches" before your appeal goes out prepare them and, hopefully, make them eager or at least willing to solve a current problem. At this point, you should give them a problem to solve. You make an offer ("Here's the problem"), and then you encourage people to send a gift to be part of the solution to the problem. Almost always, the problem should be framed in such a way that **immediate action** in the form of a financial gift is required.

IT ISN'T ABOUT HOW WONDERFUL YOUR CAUSE IS

This is not a case of meeting a donor at a restaurant or in his/her home. Direct mail appeals don't afford you that luxury. What you need to emphasize is that urgency is required. If you don't emphasize the need for urgency, you usually will have a poor response. That's just the way it works. This is precisely where some get their appeals wrong. If you believe that all you have to do is explain how wonderful your organization is and that's all donors need in order to send you their hard-earned money so that you can continue to be successful—please think again. That's not the way donors behave.

The fundraising appeals that work best show urgency and discuss opportunities. To say this another way, your appeal should discuss what might happen if support is not forthcoming. After all, donors aren't sitting at home in great anticipation of your next appeal. They're too busy living their lives. If you want a donor to make a gift NOW, you have to give them a reason to do so.

I've been asked if "success stories" that are followed by asks are enough. No, they're not enough, and the reason is because they don't focus on urgency. In fact, success stories, by their very nature, suggest that there is no urgency and even create a sense that *there's no longer a need for support*.

Remember: people prefer giving to someone who needs help or has a problem right now more than they do giving to someone who has already been helped.

True story: Several years ago, Sue and I were driving down a Chicagoland expressway and saw a car on fire along the shoulder. A few cars pulled over to the side of the highway to assess the damage. We did so, as well. We saw that there was a person in the car struggling to get out. Along with a few other motorists, we ran to his aid and got him out safely. Would these strangers have reacted so quickly and decisively if there had been no smoke or fire? I can only speak for myself when I say I probably wouldn't even have pulled over. And I wouldn't have pulled over if there were already people helping the person who had been in the accident. I think that's just human nature. Wouldn't you agree? It's urgency that gets people to act.

It's important to note here that there is a cycle when it comes to fundraising and the annual fund that includes:

- Making the ask.
- Thanking the donor after the gift is received.
- Reporting back to him or her on the impact of the gift, which then sets that individual up for the next ask.

Am I suggesting that you need a life-or-death situation to get people to do something? No, not at all. There are other ways to create urgency that you can take advantage of:

- Using a deadline. Example: "You have until December 31 to double your impact to protect our kids."

- Or a "double-your-impact" offer. Example: "Your $100 gift will help bring a cure for childhood cancer one step closer for kids ike Jennifer."

- Showing how one gift can impact a person's life. Example: "Without funding by July 30, students like Paula won't be able to experience the joy of being a part of the marching band this fall."

Try to work urgency into each of your appeals. Are there some donors who will give no matter what you send? Yes, but remember those donors are few and far between (and usually in smaller amounts). Many more need a good reason to give and to do so NOW.

THE SKY IS FALLING

If your boss or your board want you to maintain upbeat messaging, I understand. But here's something to consider: your organization was created so that it could solve real-world problems of one sort or another. By their very nature, "problems" aren't upbeat, are they? **But when the donor helps you to solve a problem—now that's very upbeat!** It doesn't have to be an either/or situation. It can be both sad and happy.

For donors to understand that they can be the solution to a problem, you need to discuss things that may be unpleasant.

Here's an example of what I'm getting at: Have you ever had a problem with your back that caused you such terrible pain that you had to see a doctor? If so, you've had the experience of the doctor walking into the room and you sitting there uncomfortably. Does the doctor immediately begin writing you a prescription for pain medication? Of course not. She will check your back around the area where you're feeling pain so she can understand where it hurts and help with your level of discomfort. My point is that you can't ignore that which is unpleasant. Stop worrying about upsetting donors. Stop being afraid that they'll withhold their support.

Your donors deserve and need to understand the seriousness of the problem. So much so that they'll be motivated to take immediate action. When you neglect to mention the need for fear that it will be too painful for donors to read about, when you fail to state the consequences for doing nothing, you aren't being fair to them. In fact, you're doing them and your nonprofit a great disservice.

> "When dealing with people, remember you are not dealing with creatures of logic, but creatures of emotion." (Dale Carnegie)

DONOR **RETENTION**

CHAPTER 14

WHAT YOU MAY NOT REALIZE ABOUT SMALLER NONPROFITS

"Some nonprofits are strong, efficient, and inherently good, regardless of their size. Some are less so. There are large nonprofits that are incredibly effective on the ground. There are small nonprofits that are impressively lean in staff and expenses, but large scale in their impact, and there is everything in between . . . evaluate an organization by its impact, not its size."

—Melissa Kushner, Founder & Executive Director of Good for Goods

Most of the time, if you read a book on fundraising, it's been written by someone who works for or has worked for a large nonprofit. Their experience is with large staffs and big goals. They may also have many donors who write five-, six-, and seven-figure gifts annually. They tell stories that revolve around the perfect meeting leading to a mega-gift or an event so wonderful that it led to many important people jumping on the nonprofit's bandwagon.

If this has ever made you feel sorry for yourself as you struggle to capture donors who will give gifts of $400, $700, or $1,000 a year, I understand. But I'd like to ask you to answer one question: Is this an example of the big nonprofit's talent and success, or is it more that you're guilty of comparing apples to oranges?

The truth is that it's more of a challenge to run a development program in a small organization than in a large one. There are many reasons for this:

1. In large organizations, more people know of them and have positive feelings toward them and their work. Naturally, this opens the door for richer and more influential people to get involved. Smaller teams have to work harder to get noticed even a little and to try and build a reputation in their community because they're not what some call "top-of-mind." Unfortunately, they lack the resources to tell their story to a wider audience.
2. Larger nonprofits have more development staff and can more easily hire people who specialize in specific fundraising areas such as event management or major gifts, stewardship supervisor, and/or grant writer. If you're a small nonprofit with a staff of one to three people, you have to do it all. Prioritizing and managing these functions is very difficult. Believe me, I get it.
3. Larger organizations often have more programs that enable them to attract a wider variety of donors and tell more stories in their various communications. In

comparison, smaller organizations must, by necessity, focus on just a few programs. Add to this the very real challenge of providing new stories and information, and, well, it's just not very easy to do.

4. Large groups usually work with donors who have much greater capacity and are willing to be more sophisticated with their philanthropy, while smaller nonprofits may work just as hard (or harder) and be as smart or smarter in cultivation and solicitation efforts, though the result may be much smaller gifts.

5. When a large and small organization share the same donor, he or she will often give more to the larger nonprofit, believing that they need more money since they serve more people or because the donor wants to give at a level that matches his or her peers who are also giving to the larger organization. A good example of this is donors who give to the community college they attended but give more to the college or university from which they received an advanced degree.

In these books, written from the perspective of a larger nonprofit, there are strategies and tactics that fit organizations that have budgets more in the range of $250,000-$1 million. Remember, getting a gift of $1,000 from one of your best donors can be as difficult to get as a $ 1 million gift. Don't forget that, and don't let your board or CEO forget it either.

A friend of mine who lives in Silicon Valley was at an event attended by a very wealthy man who is considered one of the richest men in the world. Everyone in attendance was asked to give a gift at the end of the event. People were asked to raise their hands when the amount they would like to give was mentioned. The gift increments started at $200,000. When this number was announced, the wealthy man raised his hand. When the smallest gift increment of $500 was announced, my friend raised his hand to commit.

I remember he told me that when Mr. X raised his hand to commit to $200,000, the audience rose and wildly applauded. There was no such show of support when my friend committed to $500. The rub in this is that my friend's gift of $500 was far more "generous" and sacrificial than was the $200,000 given by the wealthy man. For him, writing out a check was much easier than for my friend to write out his for five hundred dollars.

How so? The $200,000 gift came from incredible wealth and an unlimited supply of discretionary cash. My friend's gift was given in spite of his much more modest income.

My point in telling you this is that if you work for a smaller nonprofit organization, I know what many of your money-raising challenges are. Rescigno's has been working successfully with organizations just like yours for years. I invite you to embrace the challenge of raising much-needed funds even though your resources may be few and far between. Continue to keep your donors informed, engaged, and feeling a part of the important work that you do.

Make sure that you have a solid plan and are following it. Put your time and money into fundraising activities that will bring the most profit. Always put your best donors first but be sure to give all your donors at least some attention. Finally, share your vision for what you hope the organization will become because people want to be a part of something they are contributing to and know is growing.

CHAPTER 15

IMPROVING DONOR RETENTION THROUGH BETTER DONOR RELATIONS

"Successful nonprofits remember one thing: focus on donors over donations.

—Causevox

You know it, and so do I. You and your team could be doing a better job when it comes to the relationships you're building with your donors. Probably a lot better. After all, there is work involved in strengthening or growing relationships. Hard work. That's a given.

What I see all too often is that a decision is made to concentrate on donor acquisition instead of donor retention, even though the cost of acquiring a new donor has proven to be as much as five times as costly as retention.[3]

Why is it that so many nonprofits do this? If I hurt some feelings by saying this, I don't mean to, but so be

---

[3] Findtouchpoints.com. "Why Donor Retention Is Greater than Donor Acquisition," May 14, 2019.

it. Maintaining and strengthening relationships means ensuring that the donors you have are happy, engaged, and continuing to support you. Like I said, that's hard work, and it takes commitment. Unfortunately, the will or commitment is often lacking in organizations that aren't "relationship" strong. Is it lacking in yours?

For many nonprofits, donor retention is kept in the category of "top secret." After all the work your team does to acquire new donors, only about one out of five ever give a second gift. After all, the whole idea behind good donor relations is to give your supporters the best experience with your organization that you possibly can. Why? Because succeeding at good donor relations can help you win larger contributions and increase their lifetime value.

You should make it your goal to maintain good donor relations. Some suggestions:

1. ***Communicate more often*** – Even when no "campaign" is happening and certainly between your appeals, it's very important to maintain communications with your donors. These can be messages that keep donors engaged through surveys, contests, or simple organizational updates. These tactics also help in collecting vital data about your donors. So, keep your messaging diverse. Don't just repeat what you've already said. Send stories of beneficiaries, give updates that are both long and short, have both fun and serious conversations, whatever it takes to keep your donors wondering what you'll be sending them next time. You should also have a regular frequency to your messaging. These messages shouldn't be so frequent that your readers

become bored. And they shouldn't be so infrequent that there is so long a gap that you're forgotten about. Usually, a monthly or bi-weekly update is a good way to go. More than two of these kinds of communications in one week is probably too many.

2. *Focus on different communication channels* – People who are tech-smart, of different educational levels, different age groups, and occupations prefer different communication channels. From a donor's perspective, isn't it a no-brainer that communications that you send out be on a channel that they prefer and are most comfortable with? Some examples include text messages, emails, and direct mail letters. If your nonprofit simply focuses on one comfortable, easy-to-afford channel, you're risking that what you are sending will be ignored. Diversify your channels. There is no one channel that will be the answer. By combining as many as is appropriate to your audiences, you'll be going a long way toward better donor relations. Segment your donors by their preferred channel and then send them messaging through those channels.

3. *Make the transaction process an easy one* – **Beware:** giving channels with a long donation process severely harm donor relations. In various reports I have read, there is as much as a 50-70% "give up" rate for some donation pages that are too long. To be clear, that's not good. Even if a person goes through the long process the first time, they are certainly more likely to give you a second gift if you shorten the process the next time. Take a look at your donation process today.

4. *Use different templates to thank donors of different sizes and kinds* – A 2021 study showed that targeted messaging after the donation could increase

donation rates depending on past giving behavior. Did you know that first-time donors react differently than repeat donors to messages of gratitude? In the same way, a thank-you note's messaging form and size should be personalized to each person to effectively retain them. It seems to me that the biggest mistake in donor relations is having a one-size-fits-all gratitude process for donors. Think about it: donors want to feel good about giving to you. **The size of your gratitude should reflect the size of the gift. Fixing this donor relations mistake requires personalizing each message by adding smaller details such as the donor's name, the kind of donation, and the cause they gave to.**

5. *Update donors on specific causes they've given to* – In order to create improved donor relations, you must let your supporters know how their gift(s) create impact. To do this, make sure that your donors get timely reports, acknowledgments, and updates. If you are successful with this, continued engagement will be your reward. If you fail to do so, you'll shake their confidence. That's a dangerous thing, especially when you're trying to nurture donors through the initial stages of giving.

6. *Surprise your donors* – A thank you program that is "different" will go a long way when it comes to donors making repeat gifts. Any development program that spends 85% of its time on raising money but only 15% on thanking its donors can't hope to have much of an impact on its retention numbers. Timely, personal, and specific-to-the-gift thank-you letters that make people excited to read them are so important.

7. *Mention the gift's value* – Keep your donors informed on how their dollars are being used and how much those funds have helped the mission or cause.

8. ***Use a personal touch*** – If you've sent out the acknowledgment letter in a timely fashion, that's fantastic! Follow that up with a personal phone call to as many donors as you possibly can to thank them for their gift. Honestly, this s one of the best and smartest tactics you can implement into your retention toolkit. This is true even for those younger donors who say they don't like to talk on the phone.

As a matter of fact, at the Arizona Alliance for Nonprofits Conference, where Sue and I spoke in August of 2022, a young lady proudly announced during our presentation that as a twenty-four-year-old, she doesn't particularly like accepting calls from unknown numbers, but does enjoy listening to messages that are left. Here's the point: studies have been done on this particular aspect of donor retention, and time after time, the results have shown that while young people may, in fact, be averse to talking on the phone, the subliminal feelings of goodwill shouldn't be ignored. And that goes for actually speaking with someone from the fundraising office or, yes, even a message being left.

9. ***Don't ignore the donor's motivation*** – Especially with first-time donors, by all means, try to encourage a continuation of the conversation. Whether you thank them in person, via email, or direct mail, ask them what motivated them to give. If you can understand this about your donors, you will then be able to have an understanding of what they are trying to accomplish.

CHAPTER 16

DONOR DEVELOPMENT PROBLEMS AND HOW TO ATTACK THEM

"It is our attitude at the beginning of a difficult task which, more than anything else, will affect its successful outcome."

—William James, American philosopher, historian, and psychologist

Developing donors isn't easy, is it? If you're trying to raise money for your nonprofit organization and pursue new projects, you need to engage the donors you already have AND actively nurture new ones. There's a lot wrapped up in that last sentence. You can't afford to be involved in too many other things that are at the expense of donor development. The bottom line is **if you don't have a donor development strategy, you're making a mistake.**

To expand on that theme of problems, here are some others to stay away from:

- *The "follow-up" problem* – People who make large donations to your nonprofit may not be waiting for you to appear on their doorstep to acknowledge their gift. But if your staff (and that includes you) isn't following up with your donors, that's a donor development no-no.

- *The "favoritism" problem* – It's your job to make big donors feel like their generosity has been impactful and is extremely valued by your organization. You do need to be cautious, however, about how you honor or express your gratitude for that generosity. It's my experience that it also encourages other high-level gifts that are publicly met with equally high-level appreciation and end up making those who give less feel like they're less valued or less impactful. I know that is never the intention, but it's something to be aware of so that it doesn't creep into your acknowledgment process. Remember this: you should be recognizing your supporters for who they are, not what they do (or give). Why? Recognizing what someone does, raising money, volunteering, etc., focuses on short-term behaviors. Recognizing people for who they are—environmentalists, caretakers, animal rights advocates, etc.—produces long-term affinity and ultimately results in more revenue. So don't give "things" because of something donors have done; instead, give carefully for who they are.

- *The "manual" problem* – I'm sure you would agree with me that very little, if anything, can take the place of face-to-face communication. After that, hand-written notes or personal emails are a great way to express appreciation. Inevitably, though, if you try to do everything manually, things will get by you. Should automated emails be a part of your donor development strategy? Without a doubt. But those emails shouldn't replace other things you do to nurture your donors. To be clear on this point: Everyone who gives should automatically get a personal thank-you email from your staff, along with a series of messages about why their support has made or is making a difference, what your organization is doing because of their generosity, and how they can continue to be involved.

- *The "lack-of-involvement" problem* – It's natural to assume that your best and biggest donors are also some of the people who are most involved in your nonprofit. After all, they've invested the most, right? Hold on a minute though. You just might be really shocked to find out how many of your major donors don't go to small group meetings they're invited to, don't volunteer, or participate in events. Be sure to include increasing and strengthening the connections major donors have with your mission. Their donation, if you stop and think about it, is a very real sign that they want to be a part of your work. By all means, provide them with other ways to get involved.

- *• The "taking-it-for-granted" problem* – While it is true that most people don't give thousands of dollars the first time they make a gift to a nonprofit organization, your best donors very likely aren't strangers to the work you do, and they have a level of trust that you'll use their support wisely. But that doesn't mean that they know all you'd like them to about your services and impact. That is a very dangerous assumption to make. As part of your donor development strategy, include educational opportunities about your mission and the needs of those you serve. Let me say that differently for clarity:

make sure you talk about the available opportunities *that could make a difference for your beneficiaries, not for the organization.* Remember, we're talking about people who are supporting your cause at a significant level, and as they get a more complete picture of who you are and what you do, the potential that they'll agree to offer even more support.

CHAPTER 17

BRIDGING THE GAP BETWEEN GIFT 1 AND GIFT 2

A donor who makes a second donation within three months of their first has a 98% higher average value over five years than a donor who gives once.
—**Analytical Ones, July 2021**

Believe me, the gap exists. It's all too real. You may not know that it exists, but it does. Why it exists is the problem that I want to help you solve.

If you can't give me a positive answer when I ask you how many new donations you received with your last mailing and how many gave a second gift, I can all but guarantee you that at least 60% of your first-time donors never gave a second gift, which, of course, almost makes it a certainty that you lost them after the first donation.

Why? There are many answers to this question, among them "touches" and cultivation approaches. While it goes without saying that "touches" are critical, there's more to it than just that.

The key is, in other words, relationship building. Be

advised when I use these words, I'm not talking about a feeling that's cuddly or soft. What I do mean to imply by relationship building is a strong donor-to-nonprofit relationship.

The key to the relationship is in knowing your connection to your donors. What this implies is the delivery of a consistent, reliable experience so donors know what to expect when interacting with you and your nonprofit. When you fail to establish this connection, you fail. End of story. From the viewpoint of donors, after the first gift has been sent, you are in their sights, so to speak. While the donor has made a judgment about you and your cause, it's not well-formed yet.

Now imagine what you do (or should do) after the first gift has been received. This second touch or interaction can be a thank you note, a phone call, or many other things. The point is that this next interaction is different than the first one—the gift that was sent. The donor may be committed to the cause you represent but that doesn't mean that there is any reason to believe that there has been a relationship formed.

If you don't deliver a reliable, consistent experience in which donors know what to expect from you, you will be putting your chances of ever receiving a second gift in serious jeopardy because you haven't established the personal connection or relationship I referred to earlier.

Think about visiting a restaurant for the first time. You have a good experience. The food is good, excellent service, nice atmosphere, and reasonable prices. You and your partner say that this is a place to come back to in the near future. About a month later, you and your partner do, in fact, re-visit this restaurant where you had a pleasant enough initial experience. This time, however, the experience doesn't meet your expectations. The food did not taste good, the service was very slow, and the bill was inaccurately charging you for more than you actually ordered.

What are the chances that you'll be making a third visit? Probably not very good, right? It's not like this is a place you've been coming to for years and this is the first time you've had a bad experience. You don't have enough invested in this restaurant to bother going back. After all, there are plenty of other restaurants in the neighborhood that you know will deliver a reliable and consistent dining experience.

In so many ways, the second gift is more important than the first. It's been proven over and over that if you can get a donor to give you a second gift, the chances of that donor giving you a third, fourth, and fifth gift increase a great deal.

You should invest a lot of thought and effort into the experience you deliver to first-time donors. At Rescigno's, we help our clients develop new donor welcome kits as part of an overall new donor retention strategy. Our new donor retention strategy usually includes items like a thoughtful acknowledgment letter, the welcome kit itself, and regular email communications that keep them up-to-date on news and opportunities to get more involved.

Maybe you've heard this before, but it certainly bears repeating: until a new donor gives you a second gift, they're really more suspects than actual donors. Do everything in your power to turn first-time donors into recurring donors.

OTHER INTERESTING POINTS
AND STORIES TO LEARN FROM . . .

CHAPTER 18

DONOR MEETINGS AND DONOR MESSAGING

"I assure you, an educated fool is more foolish than an uneducated one."

—Moliere

W e've all had the experience of wanting to be rid of an annoying individual who drones on and on about something you have absolutely no interest in. When that person is on your TV screen, you can simply change the channel. But what about when that person is right in your face?

It could be a co-worker who won't stop talking about the new car he purchased recently or the office gossip who keeps telling you who was seen with whom after hours. The point is we often want to escape from an interaction. I guess that's just human nature. However, if you turn the scenario around, have you ever wondered if potential donors would like to avoid talking with you? Interesting, right?

I have a fundraising associate who lives in another state. He's someone I respect very much. Before he retired some years ago, he told me about working for a small nonprofit and the first time he ever made an "ask." He said,

I could tell as soon as I got to the café where we met over coffee that the man I was sitting across from wasn't exactly thrilled to be meeting with me. I realized that the only reason I was able to meet with him in person was because a prominent community member who was friendly with him facilitated the meeting. Before I could say too much, the prospect asked if he wrote me a check on the spot for $1,000, would I leave right away. Because I thought that was a decent first-time investment, I said sure. Boy, did I goof up on that one. I was all prepared to ask for $5,000 when he interrupted me. The man went on to write the check for one thousand, and as he was showing me out the door, he let me know that he would have given me up to $10,000 if I had been a little more persistent.

This guy clearly wasn't interested in the cause, and he had even less interest in spending time with me. What he really wanted to do was get rid of me as soon as he could. His thought process was how much I expected from him and how could he give as little as possible and still satisfy what he viewed as an obligation to his friend.

Though I was taken aback by this man's abruptness with me, I re-gathered my composure enough to suggest that his friend thought he was capable of giving more. For what seemed like an hour, he and I looked at each other. My fundraising training taught me to "clam up" after asking for a gift. The silence was finally broken when he finally asked if I would leave if he tore up the old check and made out a new one for $2500. I said I thought that would be very generous. As I walked away, all I could think about was the scenario that had just played out.

I read about this next story some time ago, and I've never forgotten it.

As the senior development officer of a large nonprofit, the executive director and the group's president were approaching the head of a major corporation. They had a cash figure in mind but decided to be bold and double it. If they were successful, the gift would represent one of the largest ever to their nonprofit. As it came close to the time to finalize the deal, the nonprofit's president said, "We'd like you to thoughtfully consider a gift of $............"

Let me tell you, he definitely was not expecting what he heard next. "That's not a problem at all," said the CEO. "If that's all you need, I'm in! I was ready and willing to give you considerably more."

The nonprofit had asked for too little. Seven figures worth of too little. Gulp! They left the building feeling like they had blown it. And they had.

Here's the point: while donors undoubtedly will think seriously when you ask for a major gift, the real "ask" is an amount that has been determined in advance based on what you know about the potential donor and on the answers to the following questions:

- How skilled?
- How well-trained?
- How persuasive is the person doing the asking?
- And how clear and inspiring is the cause?

If you can accurately answer these questions, you'll find an amount that's within the prospect's giving capacity but challenges their initial thoughts on what they thought they were willing to give.

SHINE THE LIGHT ON YOUR DONORS, BUT SAVE JUST A LITTLE FOR YOU

On its surface, donor-focused or donor-centric fundraising seems pretty elementary. You concentrate on the donor's motivation to change a situation or solve a current problem. You don't shine a light on what your organization wants to do. This makes sense to you, I'm sure. There is, however, an expensive and logical mistake that many fundraisers, perhaps even yourself, are making.

For example, the inexperienced donor-focused fundraiser may become obsessed with certain pronouns. They start counting the number of times "you" is used in their communications as compared to the number of times "I" and "we" appear. Just doing that will give you an indication of how donor-focused you are, but it will be a rather superficial indication at best. If you only focus on pronouns, you risk making a mistake that negatively impacts your results.

The mistake is thinking that donor-focused fundraising means you should never, under any circumstances, talk about your organization. Making the donor the hero or focus of your communications works. I've been preaching that for a long time. But doing so doesn't mean that you shouldn't EVER talk about your nonprofit and its mission.

Donor-focused fundraising has to include some messaging about your organization and its leader. Your nonprofit must stop bemoaning the fact that they've lost donors or grants haven't been secured. Donors need to hear about results and who is being served. What great work is your organization doing that will only continue if donors keep giving? Talk about why your mission matters. That's what motivates people to give. Donors respond to urgent human needs, not organizational needs. Tell your best story and people will respond.

It's important for you to understand why you need

to communicate about your cause and its leader—the person communicating on your organization's behalf. One of the major reasons why you should be talking about yourself is *believability*. Consider the fact that as much as the donor wants to solve the problem your cause exists to overcome, they don't have the institutional knowledge that you have. Neither do they have the experience working in the field you work in, and they haven't had your training and education.

We should never forget that donors depend on you and your organization's expertise in the field they are supporting. Assuming that they know what you know is a big mistake. Proving that you are the subject matter expert also allows them to build up a certain level of trust. If you never talk about your organization, you will miss out on donor dollars.

Demonstrating and proving you and your organization's expertise in the work that you do:

- Don't point out your budget.

- Don't call attention to your degrees or training.

- Don't tell donors that they should give to your cause because you're the expert.

- Don't reference awards, honors, or recognition you've received.

- Don't assume donors are impressed with statistics.

Here are a few ways you should demonstrate your credibility as a donor-focused organization:

- Explain why you do what you do. Offer background information and rationale for decisions and tell stories that are emotionally compelling.

- Explain why the work you do is inherently challenging. What is keeping you from more success? What are the struggles? Talk about what discourages you and why you refuse to quit.

- Talk about the lives you and they, together, are changing or have changed.

To be clear, I'm not advocating that you change your focus from making donors see themselves as heroes. Continue to do so while you also demonstrate your expertise.

CHAPTER 19

QUANTIFYING DONOR IMPACT

"Tell us how our five thousand dollars will make all the difference as you show the little girl . . . Tell us how our four thousand dollars will help tutor him and teach him more words to share his generosity with the world. Tell us how our two thousand dollars will keep the water on for the man so grateful for a quiet place to shower that he gives the gift of a shower curtain . . . Tell us about the woman with a bag of groceries from the food pantry who stands at the edge of the garden, intrigued by the children digging there, and says, 'I've never seen where potatoes come from before.' Tell us how we made this happen. Do not tell us how you are unsure of how you will afford health insurance for yourself as you spend three hours, on hold, negotiating with Medicaid, health insurance companies, and doctors . . . Do not tell us how you went home last night and cried because of all the things you cannot say. Instead, whisper the world to us."
—Excerpted from Amy Rich's Love Notes

D o you agree with the premise that fundraising isn't all about the money? For the purpose of this chapter, I'm assuming that you do. If you've ever been a donor, and if you're in this profession, you certainly should be. Have you hoped to and wanted to feel good about the impact you can have? Have you secretly said to yourself that you hope you won't be made to feel like what you can give (or do) isn't enough?

As I mentioned earlier, there have been times when organizations and fundraising professionals representing those organizations have made me feel inadequate. I've had the disheartening experience of being asked to increase my support to an organization that is both near and dear to my heart. I've supported this particular cause for a number of years. Let me clarify: it's not that they asked; it's how they asked. It's such an obvious mistake. It's really a shame. They ignored one simple premise, and that is that giving is supposed to be a good experience. If it is, donors will continue to give and give more. If it's not such a "good" experience, they'll stop or decrease their giving. Yet, so many organizations that I come in contact with still don't understand.

When a cause I believe in fails in this area and makes assumptions about my giving, I'm offended. Why? Because the donor experience, my or your giving experience, should be about more than you/your office or foundation reaching financial targets. What about your organization? Are you unwittingly putting doubt in the thoughts of your donors? When you ask for a gift, especially increased gifts, you must be careful to clearly explain the impact those increased gifts will have on people's lives.

Don't just ask people to donate. Don't make people feel bad about what they might not be able to do. Appeal to them emotionally, and don't forget to mention how much you appreciate their ongoing support. Tell an engaging story. Emphasize what they have achieved in meeting ongoing needs. Show them the difference they have made and can make again. If you do, they'll give. Just don't take their support for granted.

And be sure to adequately answer the core question that almost all donors want an answer to: *"Is my one gift really going to make a difference?"*

If you want ongoing support, you must show donors how they can affect a life, save an abused animal, or protect a river. Doing so is their connection to your organization. One way to do this is to break down the actual cost of a program and put tangible dollar amounts next to a piece of equipment, a bag of fertilizer, or the cost of sending a child to summer camp. And, again, "report back." For example, say your hospital has raised $150,000 for a new diagnostic machine. Some organizations mail a postcard a few days after the equipment is purchased to specifically thank those who donated.

And other organizations take the time to call their donors. As I've already mentioned, this can be a very powerful tool, especially when you're able to tell how the donor's gift will be used. A phone call opens up the possibility of a deeper conversation, too.

Your website and blogs are more ways to report back on impact. When donors log on to your website, can they see videos, petitions, photos, podcasts, or discussion forums designed to involve them (or other potential donors) and show them the awesome impact of their gifts?

Finally, show donors how their gifts matter by setting up a meeting with the people they help. On a local level, I know some shelters for both men and women that invite donors to meet with the men and women they've helped.

CHAPTER 20

CAPITAL CAMPAIGNS VS ANNUAL GIVING FALSEHOOD

"Recognize that the annual fund is your organization's top indicator of a donor's propensity to give to the campaign."
—The Winkler Group

L et's just get something straight: A nonprofit capital campaign should be an extraordinarily exciting time for any organization. It should also be challenging. I want to "call out" a certain segment of nonprofits who have the opinion that a capital campaign and annual giving can't work hand-in-hand with one another. They can, and they really, really should. There is a segment of seasoned nonprofit executives I know who believe that a campaign's impact will weaken annual fund results.

A survey of nonprofits conducted by Campbell & Company found that 91% of respondents maintained or increased their annual giving during and after a campaign. In addition, 82% of those surveyed saw a moderate to significant increase in their average gift size to the annual fund during a campaign, and not a single responder had a decrease in the size of their donor base both during and after their campaign.

At Rescigno's, what we have found is that if you use best practices, you will see opportunities that will benefit your annual fund. For example,

- *Enhanced donor education* – Since a campaign requires additional donor communication, you have more opportunity to educate your donors about the role of annual giving, how it supports ongoing programs and operations, and the different roles that a campaign plays. Be sure to stress that a capital campaign gift should never come at the expense of an annual gift. Consider asking for gifts that incorporate multi-year annual solicitations with multi-year capital asks that will double the impact or difference that the donor can make.

- *More reliable donor data* – When you go through a capital campaign process, you probably invest in prospect research. As you do so, you'll review data on existing and potential supporters. When you meet with your campaign donors, you'll be able to learn more about their giving interests and gift timing, as well as gain knowledge that will be very beneficial for years to come.

- *An increase in awareness* – While a campaign typically starts with invested board members and donors, as time goes by, that group should get bigger. By sharing the details of the campaign with more and more people, awareness of your mission should also increase. In this way, new support and re-engagement of lapsed donors can occur.

- A better understanding of mutual opportunities that enhance the goals of both the annual fund and capital campaigns will potentially bring out the best in your sophisticated donors, who will understand the importance of giving to both.

Another falsehood or untruth is that a campaign leads to staff and board exhaustion from the mission. Another way of saying this would be burnout, I suppose. I have found that those donors who give the most and are the most loyal to your cause are the same donors who, because giving comes from the heart, will give to both your annual fund and the campaign because they have a strong passion for what you do. For them, a campaign is a great opportunity to explain the increased impact they can have on something you already know they are passionate about. And, as I've said in the past, if it's true that giving makes donors feel good (as has been reported so often), what you are really doing is offering more opportunities for donors to feel even better about the impact they're having in an area they're passionate about.

Your board and staff should feel re-energized and have a new sense of purpose because, among other things, they're working together for the same agreed-upon goal(s) and take ownership and pride in the success of the campaign.

Make no mistake achieving campaign goals is hard work. It's good practice for nonprofits embarking on capital campaigns to conduct a planning study or assessment of their internal structure. If, during this process, staff recommendations are ignored, there's a good chance that there may be exhaustion or burnout on their part. So be sure to meet with them and assure them that you will invest in the support they need to be successful. Warning: It's almost impossible for the same staff to run both the capital campaign and annual fund programs. Those that have tried do, indeed, experience burnout.

Your campaign also presents you with the opportunity to meet with donors one-on-one. When you do meet with them, you should share an overview of the campaign, give any updates, and invite them on tours or groundbreakings and grand openings. If there are any naming opportunities, they will serve to strengthen donor commitment and connection to your cause.

CHAPTER 21

FOR A NEW FOCUS ON FUNDAMENTALS

"Gentlemen, this is a football!"
—Vince Lombardi, Hall of Fame coach of the Green Bay Packers, on the first day of practice with his new team in July of 1961

et's clear one thing up here and now: I am not and never will be a Green Bay Packers football fan. Chicago Bears is how I like my football. However, the above quote from Lombardi has a great deal to offer us in the way of insight into ignoring the basics of fundraising too.

You see, during that hot summer of '61, new head coach Vince Lombardi assembled thirty-eight members of his football team. It's important to understand that the previous season had ended with a heartbreaking defeat at the hands of the Philadelphia Eagles. The Packers had wasted a lead late in the fourth quarter and lost that day's NFC Championship game.

The players had been waiting all off-season to avenge the heartbreaking loss, and now, finally, training camp had arrived, and it was "go" time (or so they thought). Vince Lombardi had other ideas.

In his best-selling book, *When Pride Still Mattered: A Life of Vince Lombardi,* Lombardi walks into camp and starts from scratch, assuming the players were blank slates who carried over no knowledge from the year before. He began with the most basic statement of all as he held the football up in his right hand, "Gentlemen, this is a football."

He was starting from the beginning even though he would be coaching professional athletes who had nearly won the grand prize of the NFL. Six months later, the Green Bay Packers beat the New York Giants 37-0 to win the NFL Championship. That season began his reign as one of the greatest football coaches of all time. From that point forward, he never coached a team with a losing record.

This pattern of focusing on the basics has been a hallmark of many successful coaches. However, it's not just in sports where this strategy is useful. Throughout our lives, a focus on the fundamentals is what determines our results. The same certainly holds true in fundraising, don't you think? The fact is that without doing the fundamentals, the basic work, all of the details become useless. Think of that as you read through this chapter on doing the basics.

As a fundraising consultant, I get involved in doing a lot of proposals over the course of any given year. So many nonprofits are looking for a partner who will add lots of value to their fundraising program. And usually, "value" means adding to net revenue.

What do nonprofits overwhelmingly tell me they're looking for from us?

1. Do they ask if Rescigno's can help teach them best practices for their programs? Rarely.

2. Do they ask for the best practices of successful fundraising offices so they can maximize their chances for revenue growth? Occasionally, very occasionally.

What these nonprofits do ask is how we will help them innovate, what the latest trends are, or what practices are on the cutting edge. Personally, I believe everyone is always on the lookout for the fastest and easiest way to raise more money. I understand. That's the same with things like fitness products, weight loss supplements, and many other things. Big promises are made that offer an easy way to reach a goal that's not easy to achieve. The problem is that these new, shiny, easy things usually don't work the way the representatives for these products say they will. Unfortunately, the same goes for the fundraising profession.

Remember the ALS Ice Bucket Challenge of a few years back? I'm sure you do. You may have even incorporated it into your fundraising program. At the time, it was an amazing phenomenon. t really did ignite a philanthropic firestorm and had tremendous momentum. In the end, it was a virtual shooting star. A once-in-a-lifetime event that could not sustain itself. It was definitely successful for about a year or so.

Flashy new things are a part of my conversations with clients and prospects. A development director will say to me, "Our board chair heard about something called crowdfunding," or "My executive director wants us to raise money on Instagram." These tactics are like lottery tickets—they're nice to have as extras, but you certainly should not be pinning all of your fundraising hopes and prayers on them being successful.

Instead, you should be committing yourself and your team to focus on these best practices:

- Do you have a strategy? Is it in writing?
- Do you know which audiences are most likely to support your cause?

- Have you figured out the best way to reach them?

- Do you have a persuasive and powerful case for support that allows others to see why you do this work?

- Is there a plan for the fiscal year? Does it include schedules, projected costs, and estimated revenues? Will actual results be measured against projected outcomes and changes to your program made based on actual results?

- Do you and your staff tell stories that are both powerful and persuasive? Do they emotionally (first) and intellectually (second) engage your audience?

- Do you spend as much time and money thanking donors and showing the impact of their gifts as you do soliciting them? In other words, are you committed to donor relationships more than you are to financial transactions?

Here's a thought: the next time a board member approaches you with a shiny new idea that they want to try, present them with the above list of seven fundamentals and suggest that the search for shiny new things should happen only if the above seven are in place.

And finally, and maybe most importantly, the #1 question nonprofits should be answering is whether they make consistency and discipline a fundamental focus each and every day. You know, just like Vince Lombardi did with a football before his first practice as head coach of the Packers.

CHAPTER 22

NONPROFITS WITH NO CULTURE OF PHILANTHROPY

"You cannot mandate philanthropy. It has to come from within, and when it does, it is deeply satisfying."
—**Azim Premji, Indian businessman, investor, engineer, and philanthropist**

Let me tell you about an experience I had with a healthcare organization a few years ago. I wanted to make an unsolicited gift to them because they had done a good job in taking care of a friend of mine who sadly had passed away. It took me three attempts to get in touch with someone in the development office. The volunteers and staff were uncertain about who to call and asked me many unnecessary questions. It was almost as if they had been trained to be the filter between me, the potential donor, and anyone who was supposed to be raising money. At least that's the feeling I got.

The person who did finally answer my call was very nice, but she neglected to get my contact information after I told her why I was calling ("I'd like to send you guys a check!!!!"), even after I asked her if she wanted my info. All she did was say thank you for calling and have a nice day.

Even after I asked her about naming opportunities in honor of my friend, she still didn't take down my contact information. It gives me pause when it comes to having any degree of confidence in this hospital foundation's ability to be a good steward of my support. Suffice it to say, opportunity missed.

You may be wondering, Ron, what does this have to do with a culture of philanthropy? Well, it has a lot to do with it actually. Let me explain: In "Under Developed: A National Study of Challenges Facing Nonprofit Fundraising," conducted by CompassPoint and the Evelyn and Walter Haas Jr. Fund, their analysis identifies a lack of culture as a key weakness of the sector. Fundraising and philanthropy need to be understood and valued across the organization.

"Across the organization"—think about those words for a minute. They're really important. Everyone from the CEO to the maintenance staff has to understand the importance of fundraising and the role it plays in their organization's ability to fulfill its mission.

I'm not trying to be critical of the healthcare organization in the example cited above. Like I said, they took good care of my friend. The question is, however, how can this nonprofit's culture, or any for that matter, be improved?

Some suggestions:
- Make regular contact with your directors. Who is the main person who interacts with potential donors? Make sure the proper personnel know who you are, and you know who they are.

- The first volunteer we spoke with onsite didn't really know what we were asking for. The second volunteer that we were referred to looked through the binder at the front desk and said, "I can't remember the lady's name who does this sort of thing." The third volunteer was almost protective—"Why do you want to speak to them? I'm not even sure we have a development office." (If I had a dime for every time I've called a foundation office and the person on the other end of the phone has no idea what a development office is, I'd be a very rich man.) And I'd be extremely rich if I had another dime for every time someone in the development/advancement/ foundation office answered the phone and didn't know what I was talking about when I asked to speak to the annual fund director.

While I'm on this soapbox, let me tell you about one of my pet peeves: I call a nonprofit organization and this is often what I hear: "Hi, welcome to the XYZ. If you are looking to talk to someone in the business office, please press one. If you want to speak to someone in human resources, please press two. If you'd like to speak to someone in the marketing office, please press three. If you'd like to speak to someone in production, please press four. If you'd like to speak to someone in the supply room, please press five. If you'd like to speak to someone in the cafeteria, please press six." Finally, at long last, the message says to press seven or eight or nine if you want to speak to someone in the development department **about giving them a gift of support with your hard-earned money.** If you think this doesn't say something to the potential donor on the other end of the phone about the level of respect your organization has for fundraising, you're wrong. Dead wrong. Do me a favor: call the nonprofit you work for and listen to its recorded message. I'll bet you'll be surprised how long you have to wait before you're connected to someone in the development department.

- Take on a mindset that your team isn't as comfortable interacting with donors as you are. One of the things I'm constantly surprised by is how timid or even fearful development professionals are of their donors. Often, it's because they don't want to say the wrong thing to them. You need to help your team understand the role they play in thanking donors, whether current or past donors. Regular training on how to communicate with donors and other constituents is critical in getting this done.

- Make sure you understand why staff members work for your organization. What makes your colleagues tick? What are they passionate about when it comes to "the cause"? If you understand that, you can help them find their own story that they can share. You can also help them relate to a donor, saying, "Our donors are excited about our organization, too."

- Collect donor information, even if you're unsure where the relationship will go, especially if the donor initiated the contact. That probably means they want to start a relationship with you. You should at least have a way to follow up.

A culture of philanthropy is a challenging thing to build and maintain at any nonprofit. It requires a consistent investment of your time, but you never know when a donor will want to make a big gift. You need to be ready, and so does your staff.

CHAPTER 23

THE LOOKING A GIFT HORSE IN THE MOUTH MISTAKE

"Donors give the most when the act and experience of giving produces stronger social emotions."
—imarketsmart.com

A friend of mine who is the CEO of his own trucking business, told me recently that he had a conversation with his college alma mater about giving them a six-figure gift. I want to emphasize that this friend's gift was unsolicited. Quite a rarity. In fact, this would have been the first gift he had ever made to any nonprofit. Any organization would feel like they'd just struck gold when they least expected it.

There were a couple of stipulations to the offer, neither of which seemed to be an issue for the small, private college. Stipulation #1 – The gift was to be used to fund a very specific project of the donor's choosing. Stipulation #2 – The gift was to be additional money in support of the project and not "in place of" funds already earmarked for it. The reason for these two stipulations was because he believed that the project would be beneficial in helping to create a bank of potential employees for his business.

Here was the problem: When the college president visited my friend at his business to talk about the details of the gift, things didn't go so well. Normally, you'd think this visit was a good idea. Go in, say thank you very much, and make plans for accepting the gift. After all, who could know if additional gifts might come in the future with a little bit of getting to know one another. I think that would be a pretty fair assumption.

Unfortunately, the president of the college had his own agenda. He tried to convince my friend to make the gift to support an entirely different project. Sadly, this different project didn't interest my friend in the least. The president was persistent in his attempts to change my friend's mind. The project he was thinking of was very important to him. The visit ended with my friend making it clear to the school president what his gift was to be used for. The president left my friend's place of business without an agreement as to how the funds were to be used. As they say, you can't make this stuff up.

Over the next few weeks, my friend became so disillusioned with the president that he took his offer of a gift off the table. To pile insult upon injury, my friend found another educational institution more than happy to accept his gift and the perfectly reasonable project he was interested in funding. One can only imagine his comments to others on this school president's stubbornness and, quite frankly, stupidity.

My friend? He has the ability to make much larger gifts in the future. Who knows what his capacity to give will be in five to ten years? Remember, the six-figure gift would be his first donation ever to anyone. Remember also that it is very rare that a first gift is the largest that a donor will make to an organization.

I wonder: how much more than "just" the six-figure gift did that president lose for his school?

There are two important lessons to be learned here:

1. It's the donor's money to give, not the organization's.
2. Donors have desires that should be respected as long as they provide valid support for the work of the organization.

CHAPTER 24

THE GENIE IN A BOTTLE MISTAKE

"Luck is the residue of design."
—John Milton, poet

You probably know that 90% of all the money given away in the United States comes from individuals. Have you spent years of your fundraising life trying to raise money from foundations, corporations, and people who were "supposed" to have money? At what point in your career did you realize that if the majority of money is given by middle class people that you should be focused on them?

Do you now realize that just because someone has given $1,000 to the symphony orchestra in your city that doesn't automatically (or in any way, shape, or form) mean that person will be interested in giving to civil rights initiatives or health care concerns or education? If so, great, but I certainly wouldn't stake my (or your) career on that ever-so-elusive-pot-of-gold.

This is the time to stop hoping to stumble upon a magic potion that will take you to the promised and of fundraising success. Instead, you should be building a strong fundraising funnel and creating your own luck.

How? Well, by creating long-lasting relationships with your donors. That's a good place to start. It takes time and effort, but if you think about it, it's the very best way to build a strong plan. Fundraising success has never been built on hoping for a genie in a bottle to appear. You need to build your own luck and not just hope for it. Hope, as I'm sure you've heard before, is not a plan.

I once heard that a professional boxer prepares to fight a ten-round match by doing 10,000 rounds of training. Think about that. Ten rounds at three minutes a round is the equivalent of me being tired just trying to figure out how long that is.

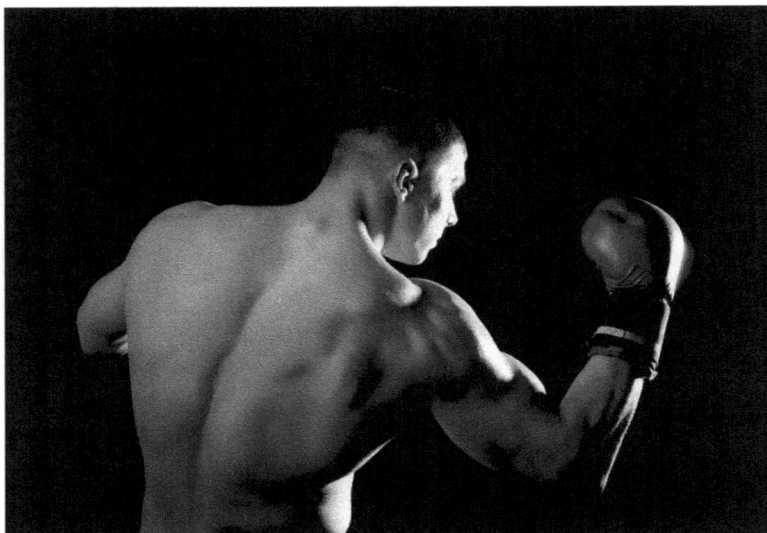

Training for those thirty minutes of boxing, then, requires 30,000 minutes of preparation or planning for success the night of the fight. In your position as a development professional, has anyone ever said to you, "If we could just get Warren Buffet to send us a gift, we'd be set," or "If only that grant would come in, our worries would be over"?

Or how about this old standby: "Let's hold a huge gala. "If we raise lots of money now, we'll be on easy street for a while." And, of course, there's the ever-present, "I keep trying to set up a meeting with that big donor, but she seems to always put me off. I wish I knew why. If she heard about how great we are, she'd give us a million in a heartbeat. I sure hope she calls me back." All of the above are symptoms of a big problem—the waiting for the "genie in a bottle" problem.

It would be really nice to just get one big check or grant or hold a huge gala and raise all the money you need in one fell swoop. You would be able to launch new programs, provide new services, or help more people right away. That's just not how fundraising success happens, however. Successful nonprofits who spend their time doing the grunt work of prospecting, cultivating, stewarding, and asking are the ones that succeed. They offer their donors opportunities to upgrade their giving. They build annual giving programs, hold in-person meetings, and make personal phone calls. **They do the work, and more often than not, it pays off.**

Have you been waiting for a genie-in-a bottle to come along? Have you put together a pie-in-the-sky plan that relies on luck, luck, and more luck? If so, now is the time to start building relationships with your donors that will be long lasting. In the end, it's hard work and putting in the time that are the only ways to build a truly strong fundraising program.

CHAPTER 25

IMPROVING FUNDRAISING OUTCOMES BY CUTTING DOWN ON DATA ERRORS

"Data are just summaries of thousands of stories— tell a few of those stories to help make the data meaningful."

—Chip and Dan Heath

I'm relatively sure I wouldn't get an argument when I say that data plays an almost all-consuming role in fundraising results. Whether your intent is to target donors who are most likely to give to your appeal or you want to track the programs that need the most resources, data analysis and segmentation are "must haves" in order to effectively operate a fundraising program. Efficiently used, data can help you know your donors more deeply, but if you get the data wrong, oh boy! What a hindrance to your growth it can become.

I couldn't even begin to estimate how many times we've been asked to start an annual fundraising program at a nonprofit and have had to pull back and say that work on the data had to be done first because, well, to put it plainly, the organization's data was a mess.

I don't need to list what I mean by "mess," I'm sure. But I'm compelled to name a few here with suggested remedies:

- *Looking at just one metric* – If you're basing the success or failure of any campaign on income alone, you should strongly consider using other metrics to have a more comprehensive understanding of donor behavior and giving trends. Consider analyzing the average value of a donation and the number of new donors or members as a broader view of metrics that could define what's working and what's not.

- *Using data to grow* – Rather than just helping you define your organization's current position, identifying the rate of any growth or decline in major or monthly giving can help you accurately predict future income and what resources will be required for ongoing growth.

- *Hand-picking the data that you use* – It's easy to sit in the catbird's seat and use data that supports the point you want to make, but it's not what I would recommend. You should use a variety of metrics for a deeper and wider understanding of the big picture so that you can make informed decisions about upcoming campaigns.

- *Disregarding what the data is telling you* – Even if you have the most up-to-date tracking system available, it's only beneficial if it's used to offer a broad range of information about donors, campaigns, and programs.

You miss out when you fail to include data in planning and analysis, and you will also miss out on certain donor insights that can help you grow your program.

- *Lacking clarity on what you really want to know* – A clear understanding of what you're hoping to achieve when analyzing data is certainly something you should be aiming for. Is it the viability of a new program or a capital campaign? Are you looking to grow your donor (or membership) base? Are you trying to forecast income growth potential over the next three to five years?

Remember, as long as you are clearly defining the problem or issue you're trying to solve, data should be able to help you.

CHAPTER 26

FAILING TO SHOW THE PROPER AMOUNT OF GRATITUDE

"Gratitude makes sense of our past, brings peace for today, and creates a vision for tomorrow."
—Melody Beattie

Think back to the last new gift your organization received, whether that was last year, last month, or last week. Let's say that you received eight new gifts last week. Fantastic! For our purposes, the amounts of the gifts are immaterial.

There are certainly many reasons that contribute to poor donor retention. One of the most concerning is a failure on the part of nonprofit organizations to express gratitude to donors for their gifts. More specifically, I'm talking about "time-sensitive" gratitude. What goes along with this is a failure to communicate to donors how their funds are being used.

In reality, this amounts to a "failure to communicate," as the warden says to members of a chain gang at his prison in the motion picture *Cool Hand Luke*. It amounts to a failure or, dare I say, a refusal to understand that donors need and want to know that (1) they're appreciated for their generosity and (2) their support is being used in a positive, impactful way.

When nonprofits proactively take a hands-on approach to acknowledging donors promptly and communicating with them regularly, their ability to retain them longer and more effectively is greatly maximized.

Can timely acknowledgment be difficult to accomplish when nonprofit staff is focused on the organization's day-to-day work? Of course. But what's more important? Retaining donors who are your lifeblood or your day-to-day work? I think you know what I believe your answer should be. Donors may say that they don't need to be thanked when they send in donations, but poor donor retention, especially of new donors, tells me otherwise. Donor appreciation and gratitude are critical. Consider the fact that donor expectations are more heightened today than ever before. This means that they expect to hear that their gift has been received and deposited within three to five days. It also means that donors rightly expect a thank you letter, phone call, or both.

If you want to ensure that a first-time donor isn't "one and done," a thank-you phone call from you or a team member is a wise retention tactic. And if you want to add even more impact, follow the call up with a handwritten note. Let it simply be to express your gratitude. Not only will it be a surprise, but your donor will know that you took the time to write a hand-written message.

CHAPTER 27

WRONGS NEVER MAKE RIGHTS

"What's the use of learning to do right when it's troublesome to do right and it ain't no trouble to do wrong and the wages is just the same."
—**Mark Twain, "The Adventures of Huckleberry Finn"**

Let me pose a question: Just because we're products of our past, does that mean we have to be prisoners of it? Whether we realize it or not, many of us look to see who is already doing something well and then model what we do after them.

When I stop to think about it, a lot of what we at Rescigno's Fundraising Professionals have learned was learned through trial and error. The hard way, in other words. Having admitted to that, allow me to suggest a shift in how you look at things. I'm sure you'd agree that there are ways to get one-time donations to raise money. The question you have to ask yourself, though, is, *does the end (money) justify the means?*

I'm a big believer that if you ask donors the right questions, they'll tell you what you need to know. That's why you should ask yourself if you're looking to reach a certain level of financial success through a few tactics or if you want to focus on long-term growth that builds a culture of philanthropy where those who play an integral part in funding your mission are viewed as just as important as anyone else.

If you believe donors are just as important, there are "right ways" and wrong ways to grow your fundraising revenue. "If you give us $250, we'll sign you up for our monthly newsletter or send you this plush puppy, etc. etc." Is it unethical? No. But how far can this kind of fundraising take you? I'm referring to auctions, selling magazines, bake sales, raffles, and so on. This approach is all wrong if you want to establish meaningful, long-term giving.

I suppose the reality is if you send "x" number of communications to a certain person at a certain zip code at a certain income level, you can expect a certain level of response. Some organizations do this very well. Again, it's not wrong to do this. However, if that's the fundamental way you're going to go about raising money over the long haul, I think you will have a problem.

EVENT-HEAVY MENTALITY

Events aren't inherently the problem. After all, they do create and foster relationships between donors and organizations that can (and should) be sustained and deepened over time.

I like to compare nonprofit events to a marriage. Sue and I have an excellent, loving relationship that has been built on years of experience, trust, devotion, communication, and so much more. Now think about a couple who are newlyweds. They are in it to stay married, right? They come back from their honeymoon and soon only spend time together on their annual vacation and the occasional work event they attend as a couple. Do you get my point? When your donors are only around for fun but not in the thick of it with you, you'll soon find that there is no substance to your relationship. To be clear, it's not a good thing.

THE GUILT–TRIP MENTALITY

"For just a cup of coffee a week, you can...." It's not wrong to do this, is it? It can be helpful, in fact. However, I invite you to consider whether you're making your donors feel guilty by doing it repeatedly.

And here's another example of the guilt technique to consider: do you ask people of high socio-economic levels to give because they've been lucky or blessed or whatever?

Two examples of this kind of thinking:

- *"So and so could write a check to cover our entire campaign and wouldn't even feel it. Our problems would be over then."*

- *"Asking him (or her) for that amount wouldn't even make that person blink."*

While this approach may result in the very occasional gift, it goes against growing the generous giving culture you should be striving for.

THE DESPERATION OF "WE'VE JUST GOT TO HAVE IT"

My best advice is to stop talking to people about what you need. The unfortunate truth is many organizations don't get what they need. Why? Because when "need" is what you talk to your donors about, whether you realize it or not, what you're doing is competing with other organizations and what they need. This approach, when practiced over a long period of time, dulls a giver's interest.

Eventually, new causes are brought to their attention, and their focus inevitably shifts.

Your mission should not feel like a fire sale to your donors. All of the above tactics may work once in a while and to some extent . . . before they backfire. They'll backfire because the ask should never be solely about the money. It must be about the people.

Recently, I read about an experiment requesting online donations to The American Red Cross. Some people were asked to contribute directly, while others were asked to donate by voting for whether they liked chocolate or vanilla best. Frivolous, you might be thinking. After all, this is a charity organization focused on providing relief to people who are in extreme circumstances. Well, what do you know, the strategy worked. People given a choice donated 28% more than those who weren't.

I have since learned that being given the opportunity to select a preference of one thing over another boosts giving simply because it provides people not just a choice, but an opportunity for self-expression. People love sharing their opinions, likes and dislikes. So, when given a chance to state a preference for a cat or a dog, or chocolate or vanilla, they jump at the opportunity to self-express—even if they have to send in a donation to do so.

This simple shift in how you make requests can have big implications for your organization. Even more topical questions about pop culture—"Taylor Swift or Adele," or sports, baseball or football. It turns out that when given a choice, even a silly one, people like to express that choice, and they'll do so with their wallets. Who knew? Well, now you do!

Focus on identifying people who want to walk with you for the long haul as you build and foster a culture of giving instead of one that is constantly groveling. One of the simple ways to do this is with nouns instead of verbs. Nonprofits usually ask people to give, donate, contribute, and help the cause. But a subtle shift can have a big impact. During the pandemic, I read about researchers who went to a school in their area and asked kids to help clean up around the school: move some blocks off the floor into a container, put away some toys, etc. Some kids were asked to help while others were asked to be "helpers." The study found that changing from "help" to "helpers" made a big difference. Kids asked to be helpers did so around a third more than those who'd just been asked to help.

Another example the research came up with was asking people to be 'voters" rather than to "vote" significantly increased turnout. And how about this one: students directed to "please not cheat" were twice as guilty of cheating as those asked not to be "cheats." It's kind of fascinating, in my view.

I know you've heard or read about the power of the word "you" (and its different forms) before. Still, I believe it's worth re-emphasizing here: Whether it's on the news ("Is there a dangerous chemical in your water? Learn more when we come back") or online ("5 Tips You Can Use to Get That Interview") the most read or watched stuff often used some form of YOU. And it's not just by chance. **"You" and its variants increase engagement.**

An analysis of thousands of branded social media posts, for example, found that the presence of some form of "you" was associated with around a 10% increase in engagement. Posts were liked or shared more and received more comments. Other studies found that songs with "you" in them are more popular. It makes sense that they work so well because they personalize what you are requesting of them. "You" makes people feel like you are talking directly to them about something that is relevant.

So instead of saying, "We need help" or "Every dollar helps," if you're looking for a donation, try "We need your help" or "Every dollar you give helps."

I hope you can see how this relates to fundraising. If you frame certain actions, like donating, as opportunities to confirm positive identities, like being a donor instead of donating, they will have more success. Ask what value your organization can offer to the donor that will be unlikely to be refused and that will help your organization. This question implies thinking about donor needs, the value your nonprofit provides, and how to link them both.

Break out of those old habits. Instead of conversations about what donors can do for you, make it about **what you can do for them.** That's right, to raise more than you ever thought possible, make the conversation about providing donors with the value they deserve and require. Ask what you can do for them in a way that aligns with their ability to help you simultaneously.

THE FUTURE
OF FUNDRAISING

CHAPTER 28

THE FUTURE OF FUNDRAISING

What does the future hold for those of us in fundraising? It's a question we constantly ask ourselves, isn't it? We live in a world where we wish to see a cure for cancer, success against climate change, and an abundance of happiness, health, and freedom for all. Any discussion of how to achieve these aims screams "technology!"

Many who work in the fundraising sector believe that bringing new tech tools on board will streamline results, increase gifts, expand the donor pool, and reduce expenses. If only it were that easy. I believe two things to be true in this regard (1) For the most part, many of today's fundraising methods are just plain ineffective. Not only that, but they also discourage new donors from giving. What a shame. (2) Regarding technology—it can be wonderful, but by itself. it cannot and will not deliver the changes so sorely needed in philanthropy.

As True North Advisory in July 2020 stated, "Technology is easy; it's people who cre hard." The writer of that blog, Scott Hoffpauier, knew a very important truth. He knew that technological advances would not solve or make up for human intangibles like empathy, active listening, gratitude, honesty, and authenticity. These qualities are so very essential as drivers and indicators of future success in fundraising, shiny new technological toys notwithstanding.

This begs the question originally posed in this chapter: *What does the future hold for fundraising?* From my perspective, it lies in fundraisers successfully bringing together pivotal human skills with key advances in technology available to them. How? Why? Well, donors still want to be seen as individuals, not as a piggy bank or an ATM. I think you'd agree with me on that point. We usually can see right through the person, or organization for that matter, who just wants our money and cares very little about us as individuals.

When a real connection is made, we feel it. I know when a nonprofit I give to has paid attention to me as an individual with my own interests, desires, and needs. I also know when I've been treated and seen as no more than a caricature of a person with cash to give away. When I feel like I have a true relationship with the person and the organization I'm considering supporting, it's much easier for me to decide to give.

New technological tools ease the cost of segmenting donors. That's true. But it often comes at the cost of personalized contact. And that's not good. When those new technologies are implemented along with authentic, meaningful relationships, that's when fundraising bliss may occur.

There are two examples of this I think will be helpful to you. They should be considered essential duties of any fundraising team: surveys and list management. Let me explain:

Surveys – About a year ago, I learned about a religious community in Texas that was described as "cutting-edge." With the onset of the pandemic, they took their programming online and experienced tremendous growth both in the U.S. and internationally. When about 500 people from outside the U.S. donated, the executive director wondered how best to engage this new audience of donors. In-person meetings were, of course, not going to happen. Instead, these donors were asked to take a short and easy online survey so the organization could learn more about them and understand what it was about the religious nonprofit that motivated them to send gifts.

The survey got a 70% response rate, and many of those responses expressed appreciation that the nonprofit even cared about their opinions. Further, several remarked that they were "surprised" that the survey didn't include another fundraising ask.

My point is that these new donors responded with ideas and thoughts that marked the beginnings of a strong donor-fundraiser relationship. The article went on to mention that this was an excellent use of technology as it was an honest, donor-specific approach that aligned with the organization's values. To put it another way, they had thought like real people valuing donors as partners. The results were heartwarming to say the least.

List Management – The same thinking should apply to list management. If done correctly, it will quickly set your organization apart from other nonprofits.

Giving Tuesday is an excellent example of what I'm talking about. I'll grant you that GT raises millions and millions of dollars for nonprofits every year. At the same time, however, you should be aware that it also makes many donors want to take their computers and phones and burn them or take a sledgehammer to them. Personally, I have often wondered why I have to be subjected to unwelcome, impersonal, and increasingly frantic emails from every organization that has my email address, emails, by the way, that ignore previous gifts I may have made or that pay no attention to my already stated giving preferences. On Giving Tuesday, the requests come hourly throughout the day. Annoying? You bet they are!

It's that type of communication and marketing that is guaranteed to turn me off. I'll bet it also makes those donors feel like the organization considers them no more than checkbooks rather than human beings. Feeling like just another name on a spreadsheet is not what you're going for, I'm sure.

I wonder as you read this, what your response is. When I've mentioned it to nonprofit leaders, the response has been surprisingly mixed. Some tell me that doing the kind of list segmentation implied would be too much to handle. Really?

I have a real concern that even if I could personally just ignore my frustration with mass GT solicitations, there are many donors who can't or won't. Taking that a step further, I'd be willing to bet that for many, many donors, sending five to seven increasingly frantic emails will foster a very negative association with the nonprofit, and that will result in donors who stop considering giving future gifts to those organizations.

As a professional fundraising consultant, I know I don't have to tell you about baby boomers passing along their wealth to millennials in what has been dubbed "The Greatest Transfer of Wealth in History." Many of these young people haven't even begun considering their own giving plans, if any. When they do, however, if they begin to feel like giving to a cause feels like they're being treated like a checkbook or they tire at the mere thought of pushy solicitations, they will be turned off to philanthropy, possibly forever.

You may be asking yourself what you can do. You can try to use technology to create meaningful, highly personalized, and informative databases that emphasize both money and capacity. In addition, it is vital to include insightful and personalized information about your prospects as individual human beings.

To sum up, I believe there are many of you reading this who truly want to make positive changes in the nonprofit sector. Part of that change is to go about correcting some of the fatal fundraising flaws I've discussed in this book. Improvements in tools like surveys and list management are just the beginning of what we will experience in philanthropy and fundraising in the future.

When you are considering purchasing new tech tools, you must also answer this question for yourself and your board: How does my funcraising office take this new tool and humanize it? Ultimately, that's how you'll set yourself up for fundraising success.

CHAPTER 29

FIN

The future of fundraising and nonprofit leadership seems always to be the topic of conversation whenever I meet with others in the profession. More often than not, the talk revolves around the right candidate for a particular position or what is needed to be ready for the future.

It makes me wonder what the next ten years will bring when it comes to fundraising.

Here's what I believe:

1. It would be very wise of you to make it about the donor and not your organization or its needs. You'll have to improve when it comes to thinking like your donors. Not that long ago, you could tell your donors, "This is what I need," and you'd have it. Today, and certainly in the future, donors won't just give because you stated that you needed a gift. You'll have to connect with them, schmooze them, if you will. This is already how donors like to be treated (and it's a very powerful tactic for your cause moving forward).

I believe in one simple truth when it comes to fundraising: there are no shortcuts. Doing the basics and doing them well is the most important "thing" you can do.

Simple things like returning phone calls promptly, sending hand-written notes, and visiting with donors to say thank you without asking for more money (that comes later). Getting to know your donors on an individual basis would be a brilliant move on your part; it really would. And listening intently to what those donors reveal to you would be even more brilliant. Why? Because it very well may inspire them to be loyal, reliable donors.

Should you be embarrassed or downtrodden about the mistakes you have made (or may make) in your career as a professional fundraiser? I think not. If you continue to make the same mistakes, of course, that's another story. After a mistake, move on. Learn from it and be determined not to make it again.

2. **Your level of confusion may grow.** Why? Simply because what worked in the past won't be nearly as effective. The new ways information flows may be overwhelming. Having someone on your team who understands this information flow could be very beneficial.

3. **It's really going to be increasingly important to focus on relationships first and foremost.** Donors are giving when and where they know what the organization is really doing. It's a tremendous advantage to your cause if you know your donors—really know them and communicate regularly and impactfully about the difference they are making through their support.

4. **Be authentic.** Be yourself. The size of a nonprofit's budget will not be nearly as important as the size of its demonstrated heart. Those big fundraising budgets that try to create relationships that turn into income are becoming more and more rare. In the future, we will all be so connected that if you're small, you can

turn your smallness into a real advantage with the relationships you form. As always, this is the best kind of fundraising—real people telling their friends about your organization and the great work it is doing.

5. **Organizational transparency will rule the day.** Be prepared for donors to be comparing how you stack up against others who may do similar work. Truthful communication will rule the roost.

6. **Is direct mail dead?** Ha! That's a laugh! However, if you're mailing to everyone on your mailing list, you'll be failing to grow or even maintain the status quo. Those who understand the power of good data will reap the benefits of direct mail ROI.

7. **Don't just look for the biggest donor(s);** look for the "right" ones. Looking for a donor who can write the big check? Ok, but you should also be looking for the one who can get you in front of the people who can make things happen.

8. **The name of the game is the experience.** Donors must experience the reality of the work you do. Whether by seeing, hearing, tasting, or smelling, help them to "feel" the importance of what you and their support does.

9. **Donors want to learn but not necessarily be taught.** Don't teach your donors about the importance of philanthropy. Help them to experience its importance by finding out for themselves. They won't continue to listen if you're not answering their questions. Answer donor questions; don't give them a sales pitch disguised as teaching them.

10. **Help donors visualize your data.** Stop working in rows and columns of numbers and lists of facts. The future of fundraising will belong to those who can see trends and bring them to life for their donors.

If you work for a nonprofit, you must realize that **money is more important than your mission.** Now, before you get yourself all lathered up with what I've just said, I fully understand there are many, maybe even you, who may not like the sound of that, but think about it for a minute. Your nonprofit exists, and its reason for being is to serve the needs of the sick, the undereducated, the poor, in general, the so-called "underserved,".

My question for you is this: do you care more deeply for your cause than you do for those your cause serves? If so, there's a problem. Successful nonprofits understand a very basic premise: their customer is their donor. This is so because if you had no donors, there'd be no money with which to make a difference or to have an impact. In other words, no homeless children would be sheltered or fed, many would go without an education, and there would be no cures for diseases, etc.

If you are of the same belief that "your customer is your donor," you must *find a way to keep them*—keep them informed, engaged, involved, and giving. Loyal and committed donors aren't born that way. What you do after the gift is received makes them that way.

The bad news is that many nonprofits have little to no idea of what it takes to keep donors happy, committed, and involved. The good news is that if you work with us at Rescigno's, we'll help you develop this survival skill. If your organization comes to understand this simple concept, it will survive inflationary periods, recessions, or come what may. Those that don't won't.

That's why I always suggest that you make donors the focus of everything you do. It's not about (and shouldn't be) your accomplishments. Make it about theirs. After all, without donors, you wouldn't have an organization, would you?

HAPPY AND SUCCESSFUL
FUNDRAISING TO YOU!

ABOUT THE AUTHOR

A colleague, after reading Ron's blogs and newsletters, once said, "He is a person I would like to have a glass of wine or a beer with. His literary voice is approachable, friendly, and has a Chicago south side feel to it. His style of writing is both unique and inviting." A great compliment when you consider that Ron doesn't drink and isn't originally from the south side of Chicago. He has written this book for fundraising professionals responsible for raising annual fund money. Ron has helped nonprofit organizations grow their base of support for over 31 years. Known as Rescigno's copyediting guru, he works with clients to create appeal letters that pass the 'donor-focused' test. In his book, he describes the process he has developed for annual fund success.

This is Ron's second book, a follow-up to *The Process-Driven Annual Fund* published in 2021.

Ron maintains a very active presence on the Rescignos.com website with his weekly blogs, newsletters, and his articles written for LinkedIn.

RON RESCIGNO, AUTHOR

ADDITIONAL RESOURCES

Are you looking to read more about fundraising? These are some personal recommendations of books that have inspired me.

- *Donor-Centered Fundraising* by Penelope Burk

  Penelope Burk has done extensive research on what it takes to be truly donor centered. It's full of important and useful information of all kinds.

- *The War for Fundraising Talent* by Jason Lewis

  This book is especially intended for small shops that find it difficult to constantly achieve their fundraising goals.

- *The Mercifully Brief Real-World Guide to Raising $1,000 Gifts by Mail* by Mal Warwick. Mal Warwick explains how you can succeed on your own as it works you through a step-by-step process of identifying prospects, crafting the right message with the right response device, and the right envelope.

- *Fundraising Strategies for Community Colleges, the Definitive Guide for Advancement* by Steve Klingaman

  Steve Klingaman's book provides practical advice and concrete steps on how to build a strong advancement team.

www.ingramcontent.com/pod-product-compliance
Lightning Source LLC
Chambersburg PA
CBHW071551200326
41519CB00021BB/6703